INTRODUCTION

Deadpool has proved to be one of Marvel's most popular comic books, mixing a sassy, comedic style with action-packed adventures that never shy away from the darker side of being an assassin.

Wade Wilson's adventures have often featured unlikely alliances with fellow Marvel mainstays such as Wolverine, Spider-Man, and Captain America, and have seen him clash with foes such as Norman Osborn, Sabretooth, and Madcap. His regenerative powers are often called into action when things get bloody.

Even after 30 years, Deadpool is still a surprising, anarchic figure as he nimbly treads the line between a loveable rogue and coldbooded killer, engaging with his myriad fans as he breaks the fourth wall... and everything else in his path!

MARVEL ANNIVERSARY SPECIALS
Marvel Comics: The First 80 Years
Captain America: The First 80 Years
Fantastic Four: The First 60 Years

THE OFFICIAL MARVEL STUDIOS SPECIALS
Thor: Ragnarok
Black Panther: The Official Movie Special
Black Panther: The Official Movie Companion
Ant-Man and The Wasp

Marvel Studios: The First 10 Years
Avengers: Infinity War
Captain Marvel
Avengers: Endgame
Spider-Man: Far From Hone
Avengers: An Insider's Guide to the Avengers Films
Black Widow
WandaVision
The Falcon and the Winter Soldier

DISNEY PUBLISHING WORLDWIDE
Text Fabio Licari, Marco Rizzo
Additional Text & Editing Steve Behling
Design and Editing Ellisse s.a.s. di Sergio Abate & C. Valentina Bonura (Designer) Tiziana Quirico (Editor)
Translation John Rugman
Thanks to Guy Cunningham, Joseph Hochstein, Mark Long, Caitlin O'Connell, Brian Overton, Jeff Youngquist.

Originally created by Disney Publishing Worldwide

TITAN EDITORIAL
Editor Jonathan Wilkins
Group Editor Jake Devine
Art Director Oz Browne
Production Controller Kelly Fenlon
Production Controller Caterina Falqui
Production Manager Jackie Flook
Sales and Circulation Manager Steve Tothill
Marketing Coordinator Lauren Noding
Publicist Phoebe Trillo
Digital and Marketing Manager Jo Teather
Acquisitions Editor Duncan Baizley

Publishing Directors Ricky Claydon & John Dziewiatkowski
Operations Director Leigh Baulch
Publishers Vivian Cheung & Nick Landau

DISTRIBUTION
U.S. Newsstand: Total Publisher Services, Inc.
John Dziewiatkowski, 630-851-7683
U.S. Newsstand Distribution: Curtis Circulation Company

PRINTED IN CHINA

U.S. Bookstore Distribution: The News Group

U.S. Direct Sales: Diamond Comic Distributors
For more info on advertising contact adinfo@titanemail.com

Deadpool: The First 30 Years published August 2022 by Titan Magazines, a division of Titan Publishing Group Limited, 144 Southwark Street, London, SE1 0UP.

For sale in the U.S. and Canada.

ISBN: 9781787738706

Thank you to Guido Frazzini, Christopher Troise, Kevin Pearl, and Eugene Paraszczuk at Disney.

© 2022 MARVEL

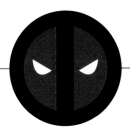

"I'M DEADPOOL, AND I'M THE BEST, IF I DO SAY SO MYSELF..."

No, hold it. No way. You mean it? You're doing a magazine about yours truly? One of those classy, full-color ones you find in bookstores? Like I'm Captain America, or Spider-Man, or an Avenger? (Here's a secret: I'm way better.) So it's true: I've become one of the greatest Marvel Super Heroes ever. A popular, best-selling, loveable, handsome, proud, daring, shameless hack… no, scratch that last part.

I'm basically the best around right now. And I'm turning thirty. Thirty years as the Merc with a Mouth, since they decided to launch me into a comic about the New Mutants, with that old barrel of laughs Cable. Check it out sometime. It was supposed to be a hit-and-run, but I'm still here. Deadpool. D-e-a-d-p-o-o-l. Don't you just love the sweet, sweet sound of my name?

I've seen it all since then. They've done so many series, miniseries, yada yada yada about me that I've lost track. They've written and drawn me in dozens of ways since those two crazy kids Rob Liefeld and Fabian Nicieza decided to "create" me. It's their fault that I'm talking to you right now, and everyone who came after them didn't help. Otherwise I'd have been spared all this "breaking the fourth wall and talking to you knowing I'm a comic book character and you're my readers" stuff. But that's how they made me.

And they gave me other talents, too. I've got a healing factor that outshines Wolverine's. I've got aim that Hawkeye dreams about at night. I never get tired. I can time travel. I've got this great red ninja suit that Spidey wishes he had (take that!). An ex-Marvel Editor in chief, Axel Alonso, said, "Deadpool is part Bugs Bunny, part the Punisher." Now, I'm not sure exactly what that means, but it sounds very cool, so I'll take it as a compliment. And I'm the chattiest Super Hero, too. I talk even more than that brainiac Reed Richards, who no one understands. At least I make sense!

My story's kind of complicated. I can't remember who I was or what my name is. I don't remember my parents—could be dead, could still be alive. I don't know what I'm doing tomorrow—or even today. But I was a mercenary, I do remember that. And now I'm Wade Wilson under this mask, which is good to have around; in the past I got so sick the X-Factor cured me but left me with a few aesthetic side effects. Whatever, I still like me for who I am.

I'm also a little crazy. What did you expect? After thirty years running around the universe, bumping into guys like Thanos, it's just impressive I'm here writing the intro to my book. And it's a great book, too. To thank the authors I said they could take some time off, told them I'd take care of it. They didn't complain. Actually, I guess they can't really complain. You see, I wasn't a big fan of a couple things they wrote, so I thought they needed a long vacation to think about it.

But relax. I've fixed the mistakes, added some pizzazz. And I've been so modest. You won't read about how I'm the best guy ever, since you already know that. But if you want to hear my story—origins, friends, enemies, greatest adventures—you're holding the right book! Let me know if you liked it after. Because you're gonna like it, right…?

Deadpool
(while Fabio Licari and Marco Rizzo take some time off…)

ORIGINS

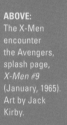

THE NEW MUTANTS

It all began with the first X-Men spinoff where, in 1991, the Merc with a Mouth was born.

Once upon a time there were the X-Men. The first mutants in the Marvel Universe were created in September 1963 by the tireless creative duo of Stan Lee and Jack Kirby—who at the time had already come up with the Fantastic Four, the Hulk, Thor, and the Avengers, amongst many other Super Heroes. The adventures of the gifted youngsters trained by the powerful telepath Charles Xavier, also known as Professor X, combined Super Heroes and adventure while bravely exploring the theme of discrimination. Lost, confused, and alone, those five kids—Cyclops, Beast, Marvel Girl, Angel, and Iceman—represent the misfits and the outcasts, the ones feared by society just because a genetic mutation gave them unusual powers.

The series got off to a strong start, but a later drop in sales forced Marvel to shut down production at issue #65—from #66 to #93 (December 1970—June 1975), the comic distributor only put out reprints. The turning point came in 1975 when, in search of a series with international appeal (with internationally diverse protagonists) scriptwriter Len Wein and artist Dave Cockrum teamed up for the unforgettable *Giant-Size X-Men #1*. The prophetic title, "Second Genesis," actually inaugurated the new season of Marvel mutants. Thanks to Chris Claremont's scripts and John Byrne's artwork, X-Men became the most commercially successful series of the '80s.

To capitalize on this trend, the Marvel Editor-

ABOVE: The X-Men encounter the Avengers, splash page, *X-Men #9* (January, 1965). Art by Jack Kirby.

RIGHT: Splash page of Second Genesis of mutants, *Giant-Size X-Men #1* (May 1975). Art by Dave Cockrum.

OPPOSITE PAGE: Cover from *Marvel Graphic Novel #4* "The New Mutants" (October 1982) Art by Bob McLeod.

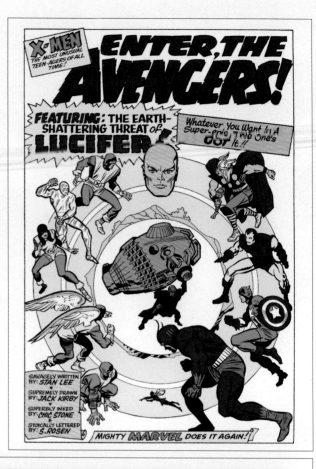

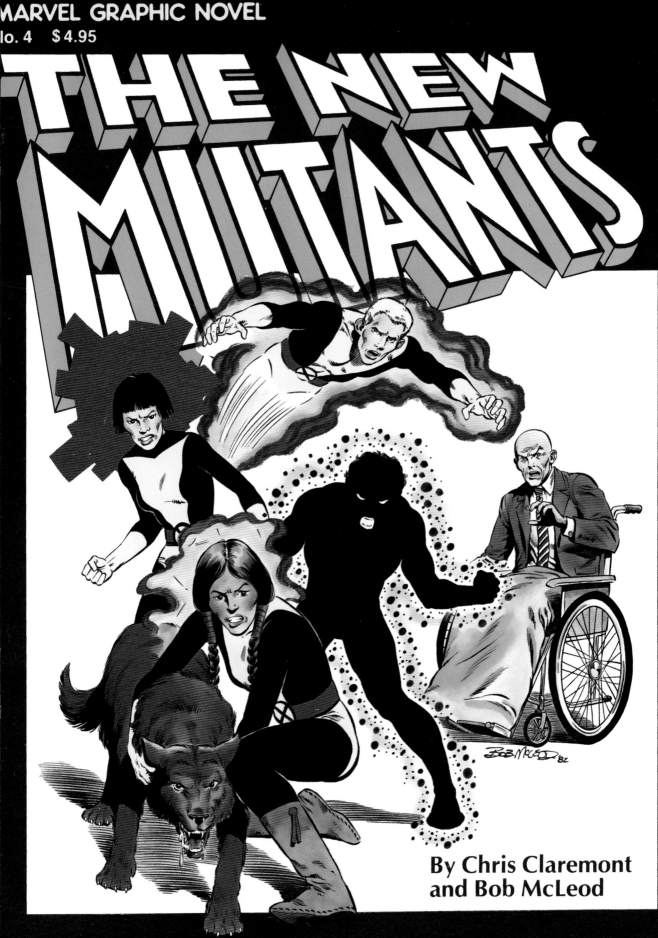

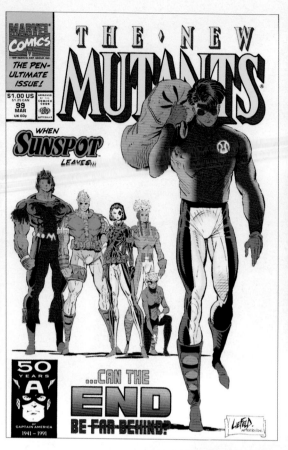

in-chief at the time, Jim Shooter, proposed a new series starring another group of mutants to accompany the main one. This was naturally entrusted to Claremont, with artwork by Bob McLeod and was called *The New Mutants.* It first appeared in September 1982 in a graphic novel from the Marvel Graphic Novel line, followed in March 1983 by the first issue of the regular series. It featured the teenage students of Professor Charles Xavier's School for Gifted Youngsters. The first group was made up of Cannonball, Karma, Mirage, Sunspot, and Wolfsbane. The public response was positive, thanks above all to Claremont's talent for depicting the group's interpersonal dynamics and teen conflicts.

The arrival first of Sal Buscema and then especially of experimental artist Bill Sienkiewicz provided the charm and originality that turned *The New Mutants* into a cult series. Claremont kept writing for it until issue *#54,* and then Louise Simonson took care of the text until *#97.* Meanwhile, with issue *#86* (February 1990), a new artist came onto the scene: the young, promising Rob Liefeld, who broke with the past and whose hyperkinetic, over-the-top style

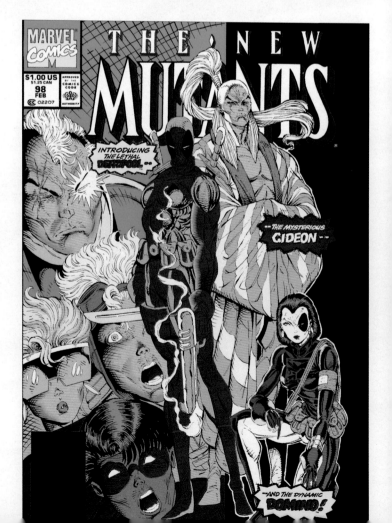

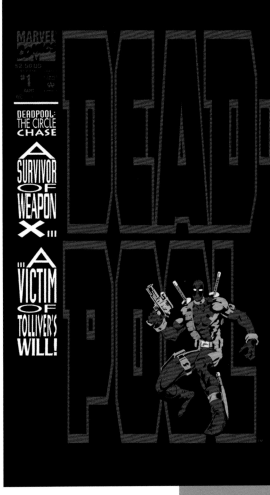

instantly made the comic book a hot property. In the next issue, *#87*, Liefeld introduced Cable: Nathan Summers, son of X-Man Scott Summers and Madelyne Pryor (Jean Grey's clone), all the way from the future, and soon he became a key figure of the mutant saga. Readers loved the new style and the turn toward a more proactive team, so in issue *#98* Liefeld was also promoted to story editor, while the

dialogue was assigned to writer Fabian Nicieza.

Issue *#98* was a historic comic, marking the first part of the final trilogy of Volume 1 entitled "The Beginning of the End" (February —April 1991). Most importantly it was the wildly successful debut of the Merc with a Mouth, Deadpool. It was a resounding success —readers bombarded the editors with enthusiastic letters. Editor-in-chief Bob

Harras told Liefeld not to forget it. In August 1991, *The New Mutants* was replaced by a new comic entitled *X-Force*. The first issue sold five million copies, making Rob Liefeld one of the hottest artists of the '90s. Soon Deadpool showed up again and his popularity led Marvel to publish his first miniseries in 1993. Deadpool hasn't stopped since. What you're about to read is his story...

"Any o' you guys lissenin' t'me?"

DEADPOOL

BIRTH

Deadpool appeared out of nowhere to "kill Cable." The mission failed, but the Marvel Universe just couldn't get rid of him.

Who could ever forget Deadpool's first appearance in the Marvel Universe? His arrival on the scene is just as powerful today as it was for readers back then. The never-before-seen character won readers over on the first try, appearing on page 14 of *The New Mutants #98*, "The Beginning of the End, Part 1." The merc showed up with no warning, wearing a distinctive red and black suit that echoed Spider-Man's outfit, and smacked Cable around. Who was he? Where did he come from? Deadpool revealed his name and why he was there: to kill Cable for Mr. Tolliver. After a brief but intense fight, he was defeated, tied up, and mailed back to Tolliver.

In theory, his story was supposed to end there—a second-tier Super Villain who would quickly be forgotten. But as Rob Liefeld revealed to *USA Today*: "He was a supporting character, but he got so much oxygen because the fans just loved him. In the era of snail mail, Deadpool was getting more letters than I'd ever seen." Once he'd finished the last page of the comic, Liefeld had a good feeling too: he liked the suit, the character, and the feel of the story written by Fabian Nicieza, the character's co-creator. The enthusiasm of editor-in-chief Bob Harras further convinced him that there would be a sequel sooner or later.

Deadpool had complex origins. He stemmed from Liefeld's dream to create his "own" Spider-Man and his "own" Wolverine, characters that he wasn't working on at the time. The artist told Marvel that the new character would be "Spider-Man with katanas and machine guns,"—almost an anti-Spider-Man. Liefeld also decided to make Deadpool the eleventh test subject of the Weapon X project, which had previously experimented upon Wolverine. These two historic models from the House of Ideas were updated with Liefeld's personality. Deadpool was given

Spider-Man's taste for sarcastic quips and Wolverine's healing factor, basically making him immortal.

But Deadpool would soon become a unique hero in his own right. He became known for his uncensored, absurdist wisecracks, cartoony style and a self-awareness about being a character in a comic book. Deadpool often broke the "fourth wall" by speaking directly to his readers, bombarding them with pop culture references and amusing quips… As Nicieza explained in one interview, he thought it would "be funny if Cable got annoyed while fighting this hard mercenary guy" because he was such a complete pain in the neck. And so the "Merc with a Mouth" was born: fast-talking and totally irritating to anyone within earshot.

After his grand debut, Deadpool was reintroduced as a minor character in *X-Force*, the series that replaced *The New Mutants*, and also in *The*

Avengers and *Daredevil*. However, it was clear he was starting to get too big for small roles. So in 1993, Marvel gave him his own miniseries, *The Circle Chase*, written by Nicieza with art by Joe Madureira (Liefeld had temporarily left Marvel at this point) which was followed in 1994 by *Sins of the Past*. Those two storylines laid the groundwork for the first regular series, *Deadpool*, which launched in 1997 and ended in 2002 after 69 issues. Since then, series, spinoffs, miniseries, and team-up stories (including the inevitable *Spider-Man/Deadpool*) have followed.

It is a success story that has showed no signs of stopping. Deadpool has moved beyond the world of comic books, appearing in TV shows, video games, and movies. After the success of the first two movies starring Ryan Reynolds, a third has been announced.

TOP LEFT: A moment of relaxation for the two heroes from *Spider-Man/Deadpool #41* (January 2019). Script by Robbie Thompson. Art by Matt Horak (pencils, inks), Brian Reber (colors), Joe Sabino (letters).

LEFT: Two heroes and their surreal discussion from *Spider-Man/Deadpool #41* (January 2019). Script by Robbie Thompson. Art by Matt Horak (pencils, inks), Brian Reber (colors), Joe Sabino (letters).

HISTORY

Jack was a mercenary, crazy, and terminally ill.
The healing factor turned him into Deadpool…
with some startling side effects.

The origins of the man who became Deadpool are shrouded in mystery. His real name is Jack—at least, that's what's on his driver's license—but his last name has never been revealed. He is Canadian, but his hometown is unknown. Who is Deadpool really? He is a character with secrets that the writers still haven't revealed.

What we do know is that Jack was an orphan when he enlisted in the army as a teenager, beginning his life as a mercenary. His father was a military man, too. The story of his parents is complicated. According to the original version, his mother died when he was a kid, while his father—who he had a terrible relationship with—was killed years later by one of Jack's friends. Then it was revealed that both of them were alive. However, an even bigger twist came when he got his long-erased memory back, and he discovered that he was the one who killed them, in a fit of madness.

That was Jack: cutthroat and trained in combat. One day, a failed mission forced him to make a dramatic escape. He took shelter with a kind couple who rescued him from a snowstorm. Wade and Mercedes Wilson welcomed him into their home, but Jack stole the man's identity. In the process he also killed Mercedes. Jack convinced himself he was Wade Wilson and went back to his mercenary career with his new identity. But fate had other things in store for him.

RIGHT:
Wade Wilson speaks "like a true Super Hero." From *Deadpool and Death Annual* (July 1998). Script by Joe Kelly. Art by Steve Harris (pencils), Reggie Jones (inks), Chris Sotomayor (colors), Richard Starkings and Comicraft (letters).

Wade fell in love—something that will happen to him a lot—with a young prostitute named Vanessa Carlysle, but when he found out he had cancer, he left to stop her from suffering. At death's door, he joined the same Weapon X project had produced Wolverine, offering himself up as a lab rat; he was a perfect candidate given his desperate circumstances. The healing factor derived from the clawed mutant cured him, but the effects only lasted temporarily. Unlike Wolverine, who was also Canadian, Wade wasn't a mutant. When it seemed as if his cancer had returned, he was kicked out of Weapon X and sent to the Hospice, the

ABOVE:
A kiss is just a kiss? With Wade and Vanessa is not so obvious... From *Deadpool: The Circle Chase #3* (October 1993). Script by Fabian Nicieza. Art by Joe Madureira (pencils), Harry Candelario (inks), Glynis Oliver (colors), Chris Eliopoulos (letters).

RIGHT:
Cover art from *Deadpool: The Circle Chase #4* (November 1993). Art by Joe Madureira.

15

facility where the sadistic doctor Emrys Killebrew and his assistant Ajax subjected "failed" heroes (just like Wade) to their cruel experiments without the Canadian government's knowledge.

Killebrew tortured him repeatedly, but Ajax was jealous of the new arrival's personality and sense of humor. Wade suffered the abuse and experiments with a smile on his face, becoming the other inmates' idol. Even Death, the abstract entity that embodies the end of life, was smitten. So Ajax decided to kill him by pulling his heart out. He survived, thanks to the reawakening of his healing factor, which was seemingly more powerful than Wolverine's. After his heart regenerated, Wade killed Ajax. Wade gave himself a new name taken from a term that the prisoners of the Hospice used when they bet on when it would be their turn to die: "Deadpool."

Unfortunately, the side effects of the experiment surfaced in a horrible way. Wade was physically disfigured, covered in cancer scars, and seemed mentally unstable, with multiple personalities in his head.

From that point on Deadpool had a red and black suit, designed

ABOVE: A dance with Death and a more dramatic page from *Deadpool and Death Annual* (July 1998). Script by Joe Kelly. Art by Steve Harris (pencils), Reggie Jones (inks), Chris Sotomayor (colors), Richard Starkings and Comicraft (letters).

FAR RIGHT: A kiss with Death! From *Deadpool and Death Annual* (July 1998). Script by Joe Kelly. Art by Steve Harris (pencils), Reggie Jones (inks), Chris Sotomayor (colors), Richard Starkings and Comicraft (letters).

OPPOSITE PAGE TOP: Deadpool and Vanessa Carlysle/Copycat: it's never easy. From *Deadpool: The Circle Chase #4* (November 1993). Script by Fabian Nicieza. Art by Joe Madureira (pencils), Harry Candelario (inks), Glynis Oliver (colors), Chris Eliopoulos (letters).

by his friend Weasel, which covered his entire body. He was not a Super Hero, but rather a Super Villain, with his first allies being other criminals, such as Hammerhead, Kingpin, Wizard, and Taskmaster. His attempt to join the good guys—the Canadian group

Alpha Flight — didn't go well. Instead, it was the shady Tolliver, a Super Villain born in an alternate future, who hired him and told him to kill Cable. But the X-Men intervened and helped Cable, and Deadpool was mailed back to Tolliver.

These were the events in

The New Mutants #98 — "introducing the Lethal Deadpool," as it said on the cover. The Merc with a Mouth had now entered the Marvel Universe.

"I'm Deadpool. Pleased to meet you," he told Cable, and he hasn't shut up since.

> *"AAAAAAAGHHH!! Packing chips! That's the greatest weapon on the face of the planet."*

DEADPOOL

SUPERPOWERS

He's immortal, immune to disease, superfast, and an expert marksman. But Deadpool's most powerful weapon might be his words, which can kill.

Deadpool's greatest superpower is words. It's no accident he's called the Merc with a Mouth. He could defeat his enemies by burying them in speech bubbles or forcing them to run away just to avoid his rants.

But Deadpool has other abilities to use against the Super Villains who *are* resistant to his endless chatter—starting with his Wolverine-derived healing factor, which is even more powerful since it not only regenerates tissue and heals wounds, but also grows back organs and missing limbs. Other extraordinary gifts derived from this X-Factor include the fact that Deadpool is immune to disease, as evidenced by his cancer recovery. In fact, the Titan warlord Thanos was so jealous of Lady Death's affection for Deadpool that he cursed him with immortality so they would never meet. Deadpool is also resistant to telepathic powers—no bad thing, since he's had to deal with quite a few mutants, although Shadow King managed to mind-control him.

Deadpool is also really strong and a master of martial arts. He is an expert with pistols and the katanas he carries on his back, boasting an aim that rivals Bullseye, Hawkeye, and the Swordsman. He is flexible, superfast, and, best of all, he has superhuman stamina, so he almost never gets tired— at most he gets bored. He speaks several languages, including Japanese, Pashto, and Urdu. Last but not least, he is unpredictable because even he doesn't know what he is about to do next, let alone his enemies. Almost unbeatable, right?

RIGHT: Thanos is jealous of Wade because Death "seems to love" him. "Consider yourself cursed" is Thanos's advice to the Merc with a Mouth. From *Deadpool #64* (May 2002). Script by Frank Tieri Art by Georges Jeanty (pencils), Walden Wong (inks), Color Dojo (colors), Dave Sharpe (letters).

ABOVE: An autopsy from *Cable & Deadpool #13* (March 2005), "A Murder in Paradise." Script by Fabian Nicieza. Art by Patrick Zircher (pencils), M3th (inks), Gotham (colors), VC's Cory Petit (letters).

LEFT: Deadpool meets the Juggernaut (and it's not a pleasure) from *Deadpool #4* (November 1994). Script by Mark Waid. Art by Ian Churchill and Ken Lashley (pencils), Bud LaRosa, Tom Wegrzyn, Philip Moy and W.C. Carani (inks), Dana Moreshead and Mike Thomas (colors), Richard Starkings (letters).

LISTEN, ME AN' CABLE ARE BUDS, BUT WE DON'T ALWAYS HAVE TO AGREE.

SO YOU THINK THE SUPERHUMAN REGISTRATION ACT IS ACCEPTABLE?

GOT NO SECRET I.D.

I WAS MILITARY, THEN A COVERT OPS. IT AIN'T ABOUT WHO YOU ARE, IT'S ABOUT WHAT YOU DO.

WHY CAN'T YOU DO WHAT YOU DO WITH EVERYONE KNOWING YOU'RE REALLY *COOPER PEYTON?*

RIGHT:
Daredevil versus the Merc with a Mouth. *Cable & Deadpool* #30 (September 2006). Script by Fabian Nicieza. Art by Staz Johnson (pencils), Klaus Janson (inks), Gotham (colors), Dave Sharpe (letters).

OPPOSITE PAGE:
Deadpool in trouble from *Cable & Deadpool* #30 (September 2006). Script by Fabian Nicieza. Art by Staz Johnson (pencils), Klaus Janson (inks), Gotham (colors), Dave Sharpe (letters).

WHY CAN'T I DO IT

WITHOUT PEOPLE

KNOWING THAT?

WEAPON X, DEPARTMENT K

The secret lab where it all began.

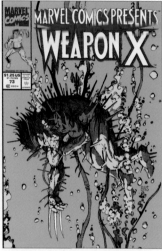

ABOVE: Cover from *Marvel Comics Presents #73* (March 1991). Art by Barry Windsor-Smith.

MIDDLE: Cover from *Marvel Comics Presents #74* (April 1991). Art by Barry Windsor-Smith.

BOTTOM: Cover from *Marvel Comics Presents #77* (May 1991). Art by Barry Windsor-Smith.

BOTTOM RIGHT: Wolverine is in pain during the Weapon X experiment. *Marvel Comics Presents #84* (September 1991). Script and art by Barry Windsor-Smith (pencils, inks, letters) and Jim Novak (letters).

There are many different ways to get superpowers in the Marvel Universe. The "luckiest" ones are mutants, born with an X-Gene that unlocks their powers in puberty. Others get their powers from accidents involving radioactive material, trips into space, or alien artifacts. Then there are the ones who get superpowers from government experiments. These include famous characters such as Captain America, Wolverine, and Deadpool. Over the years, many writers have tried to tie together all of these backstories.

Cap was the first "Super Soldier," the result of a successful attempt to upgrade a human being by turning him into a living weapon. But the process called "Project: Rebirth" could no longer be carried out after the death of the scientist who knew its secrets, Dr. Abraham Erskine. In the years that followed, the Weapon Plus Program tried multiple times to repeat the procedure that had turned puny Steve Rogers into Captain America.

The most famous iteration of the Weapon Plus Program was the tenth, Weapon X, which bonded Adamantium to the bones of the mutant called Logan, turning him into an unstoppable force. Years later, the Canadian Department K found a way to replicate Wolverine's healing factor and apply it to other test subjects. One of them was Wade Wilson, a mercenary with terminal cancer ready to do anything for a cure. At the start, at least, it looked like the experiment was a success and Wade joined the government team called Weapon P.R.I.M.E. But later the cancer came back in full force, and Wade was sent to the Hospice. This was a facility directed by Dr. Killebrew, where all the Weapon X Program "rejects" ended up. Wade was subjected to other cruel experiments there… until he rebelled, escaped, and started his new life as Deadpool. Over the years, Deadpool has run into other Department K survivors, like the government agent Garrison Kane and the violent Slayback.

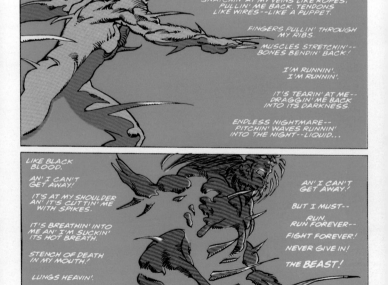

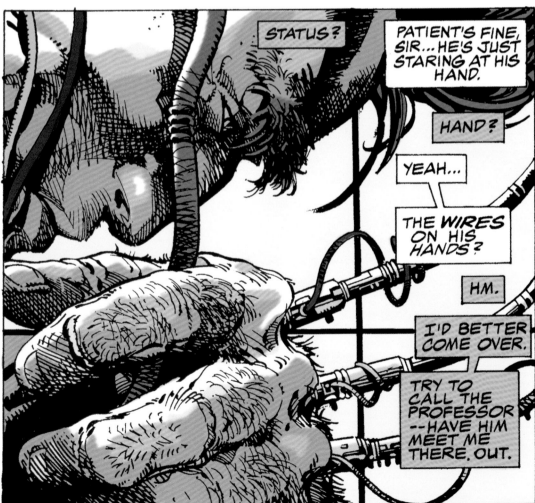

LEFT: The return of Slayback! From *Deadpool: The Circle Chase* #4 (November 1993). Script by Fabian Nicieza. Art by Joe Madureira (pencils), Harry Candelario (inks), Glynis Oliver (colors), Chris Eliopoulos (letters).

FAR LEFT: Wolverine is a resilient guinea pig, *Marvel Comics Presents* #77 (May 1991). Script and art by Barry Windsor-Smith (pencils, inks, letters) and Jim Novak (letters).

BOTTOM LEFT: The Adamantium is bonded into Logan's bones. *Marvel Comics Presents* #74 (April 1991). Script and art by Barry Windsor-Smith (pencils, inks, letters) and Jim Novak (letters).

23

ALLIES

CABLE

Deadpool's long-suffering frenemy, whose story will make your head spin!

Once there was a kid called Nathan Summers. A newborn like any other, but with an unusual family background and an even more complicated future ahead! Nathan was actually the son of Scott Summers, aka Cyclops, the leader of the X-Men and Madelyne Pryor, an aircraft pilot, who were wed shortly after the death of Jean Grey, Scott's old flame. Jean was corrupted by the Phoenix Force, an ancient cosmic energy in the form of a fiery bird (as seen in Chris Claremont and John Byrne's famous Dark Phoenix Saga). Madelyne (or Maddie) looked remarkably like Jean, which may have had something to do with why Scott fell in love with her, and when she gave birth to Nathan, the couple's life changed radically in ways no one expected.

Later on Jean came back to life — actually, it turned out she'd never died, and the version her who had was merely the personification of the Phoenix. Abandoned by Scott, Maddie went to live with the other X-Men, but later on little Nathan was kidnapped by the evil Mister Sinister's Marauders. To save her child, Madelyne made a pact with a demon and became the evil Goblin Queen. In the 'Inferno Saga,' the Goblin Queen wreaked havoc in Manhattan and it took the combined forces of the X-Men and their allies to stop her. It was also revealed that she was a clone of Jean, created in a lab by Mister Sinister, who had been interested in the Summers family gene pool for some time. Once Mister Sinister and Maddie were defeated, Nathan was given to his father and Jean.

ABOVE:
The X-Men welcome baby Nathan. *Uncanny X-Men #201* (January 1986). Script by Chris Claremont. Art by Rick Leonardi (pencils), Whilce Portacio (inks), Glynis Oliver (colors), Tom Orzechowski (letters).

RIGHT: Cover for *X-Force Omnibus* (February 2013). Art by Rob Liefeld.

OPOSITE PAGE: Cover for *Cable #35* (September 1996). Art by Ian Churchill & Scott Hanna.

Not long after, Apocalypse infected Nathan with a techno-organic virus for mysterious reasons. To cure him, Cyclops sent him to live with the Askani, warrior priestesses from the future. Little Nathan grew up there and became a young warrior, guided his adoptive parents, Slym and Redd, who were actually Scott and Jean—their consciousnesses had been transported into new bodies in the future. Like Jean, Nathan had telepathic and telekinetic powers, but he mostly used them to keep the techno-organic virus under control after it had taken over his left arm and part of his face. In the years that followed, Cable fought to save the future from the immortal Apocalypse's control… until he decided to travel back in time and stop the villain by changing the past.

Now a battle-hardened warrior, Cable travelled back in time to around the era when he had been sent to the future as a baby. That's when he turned the team called the New Mutants into the paramilitary X-Force (as told in Rob Liefeld's stories). Nathan soon crossed paths with Deadpool. Wade actually made his debut working for Tolliver, an arms dealer who was hiding the fact that he was Cable's son. Tolliver had also come from the future, with the aim of killing his father. Cable and Deadpool fought each other for years… until they were infected by the shape-shifting Façade Virus, released by a terrorist organization. The virus bonded the two of them physically in one body, mixing their DNA, and they were forced to have several adventures together, often as allies, sometimes as enemies.

In this period, covered in the series *Cable & Deadpool*, Nathan was at the height of his powers and tried to position himself as a world leader, first creating the technological utopia Providence, and then governing Rumekistan after leading the resistance. Despite the constant tension between them, Nathan and Wade formed a complicated kind of friendship. Even when Stryfe, Cable's evil clone, tried to force Wade to kill his old friend, the Merc with a Mouth managed to avoid it. Recently, Cable was killed by a younger version of himself. According to the old Nathan's wishes, his body was given to Deadpool!

TOP RIGHT:
Cover for *Cable & Deadpool #1* (May 2004). Art by Rob Liefeld.

BOTTOM RIGHT:
Cable and Deadpool travel in time together in *Despicable Deadpool #290* (February 2018). Script by Gerry Duggan. Art by Scott Koblish (pencils, inks), Nick Filardi (colors), Joe Sabino (letters).

"Blow my mind! If it isn't Nathan Dayspring Askani' Son Summers Cable Soldier X! Or are you just calling yourself Priscilla now?"

DEADPOOL

X-FORCE

A team to be reckoned with... especially if your name is Deadpool.

The fates of X-Force and Deadpool are forever bound together. Wade made his first appearance in *The New Mutants #98*, in the saga that would bring the historic series to a close and turn it into *X-Force*. In fact, the character later appeared in the series, where he fought various members of the group, like Cable, Domino, and Shatterstar. Jump ahead a few years and Deadpool was, for all intents and purposes, a member of X-Force. That's right, the mutant task force was so desperate they had to ask the Merc with a Mouth for help!

In fact, the name 'X-Force' has been used by several different teams over the years. For a long time it was linked to the team born from the ashes of the New Mutants and led by Cable. Then, for a little while, a team of bizarre mutants with showbiz ambitions "bought" the name, later giving it up and calling themselves X-Statix.

Years later, it was Cyclops, the leader of the X-Men, who founded a new X-Force. In a moment of crisis for the mutant race, he asked Wolverine to create a task force with with a license to kill, which could take proactive measures to stop the threats to Homo superior. In the battle against the evil Stryfe recounted in the 'Messiah War' saga, Deadpool fought alongside Cable and X-Force to save little Hope, believed to be the mutants' "messiah." Later on, Logan recruited his old frenemy Deadpool for a new X-Force team, knowing he was the right guy for high-risk missions. This new team was headed by Logan and Warren "Archangel" Worthington III, a founder of the X-Men tormented by his dark side. Other members included the telepathic ninja Psylocke and the mysterious Fantomex, who was also subjected to strange experiments and had a number of powers. It was Fantomex who presented X-Force with a moral dilemma on one of their first missions. He killed a child clone of the evil mutant Apocalypse, while the rest of the team was still debating if it was morally justified. Fantomex, unbeknown to the rest of the team, collected a sample of the child's blood to create a new clone, free of Apocalypse's evil legacy.

ABOVE:
Cover for *X-Statix #1* (September 2002). Art by Mike Allred & Laura Allred.

RIGHT:
Cover for *Uncanny X-Force #1* (December 2010). Art by Esad Ribic.

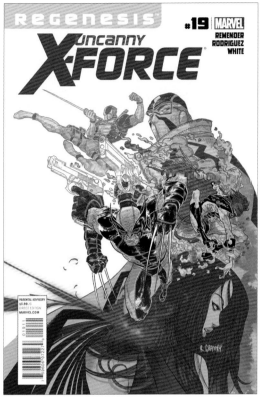

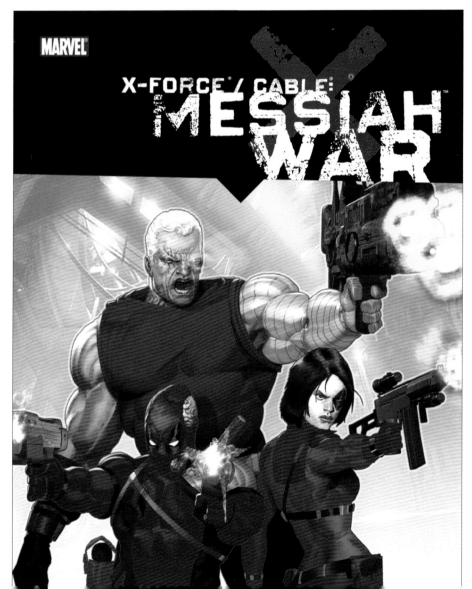

ABOVE:
Cover for
*Uncanny
X-Force #19*
(February 2012).
Art by Rafael
Grampa.

ABOVE RIGHT:
Cover for
*Uncanny
X-Force #4*
(March 2011).
Art by
Esad Ribic.

RIGHT:
Cover for
*X-Force/Cable:
Messiah War
HC* (August
2009). Art by
Ariel Olivetti.

ABOVE:
Deadpool
faces long
time frenemy
Domino.
*X-Force/Cable:
Messiah War
#1* (May 2009).
Script by Craig
Kyle & Chris
Yost. Art by
Mike Choi
(pencils, inks),
Sonia Oback
(colors), Cory
Petit (letters).

RIGHT:
An evil Iceman
freezes
Deadpool to
death. *Uncanny
X-Force #16*
(December
2011). Script by
Rick Remender.
Art by Jerome
Opeña (pencils,
inks), Dean
White (colors),
Cory Petit
(letters).

**OPPOSITE
PAGE:** Cover art
for *X-Force #18*
(May 2021). Art
by Rob Liefeld.

This incident had a big impact on
Deadpool's sense of guilt, but he was
finally welcomed into the ranks of an
X-team (after trying and trying to get
in!) and able to continue on his path to
redemption. That doesn't mean Wade
held back when he got the chance to
kill his enemies while he was part of
X-Force, though.

For example, he saved the rest of
the group from the scientist known
as Father, who triggered a future
Armageddon with his Deathlok army.
But during his time in X-Force,
Deadpool got what was coming to
him, too! In the 'Dark Angel Saga,'
an Archangel corrupted by Apocalypse
tried to conquer the world along with
his "Horsemen" and evil versions of the
X-Men from another dimension. An
evil Iceman froze Wade and shattered
him. Deadpool only came back to
life after his allies literally picked up
the pieces. To this day, X-Force is the
group Wade has fought in the longest.
Although the team's missions were
often far from noble, and not even
close to the X-Men's mission of peace,
X-Force marked an important moment
on Wade's path to redemption. For
once, instead of fighting for money,
he was fighting for a cause.

NICK FURY

War hero, secret agent, and director of S.H.I.E.L.D.
Ally to all Marvel Super Heroes, even the Merc with a Mouth!

There's probably no character in the Marvel Universe with more crossovers than Nick Fury. Nicholas Joseph "Nick" Fury often intervenes in key moments in the lives of Super Heroes — from the Fantastic Four, to Spider-Man and Captain America, he always brings action, adventure... or problems.

After spending years as a soldier and secret agent, Fury became the director of the government spy organization S.H.I.E.L.D. By now the cigar-chomping hero's voice was hoarse from his decades of smoking and barking orders, and he also wore a patch over his left eye. It was inevitable that someday he would run into Deadpool one day. Their meeting occurred during a very dramatic event: the terrible invasion.

In the story arc 'One of Us,' Fury gave Deadpool the job of infiltrating the Skrull base on Mount Cheyenne to hack into the computers and retrieve the biological data needed to defeat Queen Veranke and the alien army. Later, Norman Osborn would ruin Deadpool's plans (we'll see how), but the fact that Fury turned to a cold-blooded, amoral killer like our favorite mercenary shows just how serious the situation was. Earth was at real risk of being conquered by this alien warrior civilization, and someone like Deadpool would be more believable as a possible Skrull ally than a "good guy."

Created in 1963 by Stan Lee and Jack Kirby in *Sgt. Fury and his Howling Commandos*, Fury fought in World War Two at the head of an elite international task force, also helping

Captain America fight the Nazis. As Fury attempted to throw a grenade back at the enemy in order to save his men, it exploded, destroying his left eye, and he's worn a patch over it ever since.

Lee and Kirby brought Fury into the present day in *Fantastic Four #21*

(December 1963), revealing how the hero joined the CIA after the war, achieving the rank of colonel. Later on, in stories inspired by James Bond, Fury became the leader of S.H.I.E.L.D. in graphic artist Jim Steranko's memorable run of stories starring the character.

LEFT: Cover from *Sgt. Fury #1* (May 1963), first appearance of the Sergeant. Art by Jack Kirby.

OPPOSITE PAGE TOP: Deadpool travels to the past in "Death Comes to Tinseltown (or The Last Hitler)" and encounters... the Führer. From *Deadpool #26* (March 2014). Script by Gerry Duggan, Brian Posehn. Art by Scott Koblish (pencils, inks), Val Staples (colors), Joe Sabino (letters).

ALLIES

34

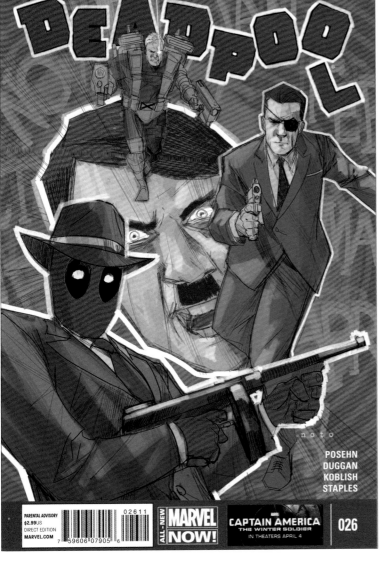

Fury has no real superpowers, but he ages very slowly thanks to the Infinity Formula he's been taking since the '40s. Deadpool and Fury proved to be a popular combination with Marvel writers.. In 'Death Comes to Tinseltown, or The Last Hitler' (*Deadpool #26*, 2014), the mercenary actually time traveled to save the sergeant from an attempted murder by the evil Führer himself.

In recent years Fury has often been at the center of the main Marvel continuity, thanks, in-part,

BELOW: Cover from *Deadpool #26* (March 2014), "Death Comes to Tinseltown (or The Last Hitler)". Art by Phil Noto.

to his cinematic comeback. In 2012 he found out that he had a son, Nick Jr., the product of his relationship with Nia Jones, who had been kept secret to protect him from Fury's enemies. The young man, modeled on the big-screen Fury (played by Samuel L. Jackson), also became an agent of S.H.I.E.L.D. and had the age-slowing factor in his DNA.

The most surprising development came with Jason Aaron and Mike Deodato Jr.'s crossover *Original Sin* (2014). In this storyline, the older Nick confesses to being Uatu the Watcher's assassin. As he takes Uatu's place under the name of the Unseen, the effects of the age-slowing formula begin to wear off. We have the impression that we'll see him again, sooner or later, alongside Deadpool.

OPPOSITE PAGE: Splash page from "Death Comes to Tinseltown (or The Last Hitler)", *Deadpool #26* (March 2014). Script by Gerry Duggan, Brian Posehn. Art by Scott Koblish (pencils, inks), Val Staples (colors), Joe Sabino (letters).

ABOVE LEFT: Deadpool meets the Skrulls. From *Deadpool #2,* "One of Us" (November 2008). Script by Daniel Way. Art by Paco Medina (pencils), Juan Vlasco (inks), Marte Gracia (colors), Chris Eliopoulos (letters).

ABOVE AND BELOW LEFT: The amazing ally of Deadpool: Nick Fury. From *Deadpool #2* and *#3* "One of Us" (November-December 2008). Script by Daniel Way. Art by Paco Medina (pencils), Juan Vlasco (inks), Marte Gracia (colors), Chris Eliopoulos (letters).

SPIDER-MAN

The friendly neighborhood Spider-Man has a complicated relationship with the katana-crazy Deadpool.

In the '90s, Spider-Man was a little less ironic and wisecracking than in the time of Stan Lee and John Romita Sr. He fired fewer verbal shots, quipped a little less, and he was happily married. He had basically become more serious and adult. That's why, when he was looking for inspiration for Deadpool, Rob Liefeld thought of our friendly neighborhood Spider-Man: he wanted to get back that irony and need to make fun of the Super Villain du jour (while punching him out) that the wall crawler's stories had lost. A Spider-Man with katanas and pistols, but more of a jackass. Even Deadpool's red-and-black costume, spiderwebs aside, wasn't all that different. And can we talk alliteration? Peter Parker, Wade Wilson…

Spider-Man first appeared August 1962 in *Amazing Fantasy #15*, an anthology series that should have ended with that same issue. In the comic his creators, Stan Lee and Steve Ditko, told his incredible origin. It was the story of Peter Parker, a nerdy student whose life changed completely the day

a radioactive spider bit him, granting him incredible powers and a lifelong responsibility. Obsessed with the power and money he might acquire, the shy student forgets the lessons he's been taught by his Uncle Ben and Aunt May, who adopted him after his parents' death — and he's punished for it. When he lets a thief get away, the man breaks into Peter's house and kills his uncle. Peter learns in the most tragic way possible that with great power comes great responsibility.

Lee and Ditko enhanced the story of Peter/Spider-Man with an extraordinary cast of supporting characters, from the editor of the *Daily Bugle* (and Spider-Man's archnemesis) J. Jonah Jameson to secretary (and Peter's first girlfriend) Betty Brant; from his bullying classmate Flash Thompson to his friends Liz Allan, Gwen Stacy (who would go on to become his girlfriend before her tragic death), and then there was Mary Jane Watson, his future wife. And his enemies, from Dr. Octopus, Lizard, Kraven, and the Sandman all the way to the most horrible and lethal of them

all: Green Goblin, whose mask hides the rich (and unhinged) Norman Osborn, father of Peter's best friend, Harry. When Ditko left Marvel, new artist John Romita Sr. gave Peter his definitive image as a more charismatic and quip-happy hero.

Over the course of sixty years of stories, there were weddings and betrayals, and births and deaths. Along the way he frequently collaborated with other Super Heroes in titles such as *Marvel Team-Up*. Many writers and artists have helped turn Spider-Man into one of the most complicated and mature characters in the history of comics. Gerry Conway, Roger Stern, J.M. De Matteis, Peter David, J.M. Straczynski, Sal Buscema, Gil Kane, Mike Zeck, Todd McFarlane (who came up with the "spaghetti-webbing"), John Byrne, Ross Andru, Mark Bagley, John Romita Jr., Humberto Ramos… He's a true icon of pop culture, appearing in countless movies and cartoons— including Oscar-winning titles like *Spider-Man: Into the Spider-Verse*.

Naturally, the wall-crawler and

OPPOSITE PAGE:
"Just. Shut. Up!" Even Spidey is tired of the endless stream of words from the Merc with a Mouth. And it's just the start… *Spider-Man/ Deadpool #1* (March 2016). Script by Joe Kelly. Art by Ed McGuinness (pencils), Mark Morales (inks), Jason Keith (colors), Joe Sabino (letters).

Deadpool had to cross paths… and they did, multiple times. In 2016, the two co-starred in their own series entitled (naturally) Spider-Man/Deadpool, in which they shared a hilarious, quip-laden rapport. The title would run for fifty issues. There couldn't be two characters more

different from each other, and maybe that was the reason it was such a success. In the comic, Spider-Man is pretty horrified by the Merc's morals, although he gets to know the man behind the mask better over the course of their adventures. For his part, Deadpool learns some "ethics" from

being around Spider-Man. In the end, one is still a Super Hero with a strict moral code, the other an anti-hero with very few morals. The only thing that unites them is their love of words—and the fact that they have both had enormous success in print, TV and film.

RIGHT:
Spidey and Deadpool in big, big trouble. *Spider-Man/Deadpool #1* (March 2016). Script by Joe Kelly. Art by Ed McGuinness (pencils), Mark Morales (inks), Jason Keith (colors), Joe Sabino (letters).

OPPOSITE PAGE:
Cover *Spider-Man/Deadpool #1* (March 2016). Art by Ed McGuinness, Mark Morales, Marte Gracia.

"I thought if I hung with you, doing the next right thing, I could earn it [being a hero]… And maybe your respect, too."

DEADPOOL

CAPTAIN AMERICA

What does the all-American hero have in common
with the Merc with a Mouth?

ABOVE:
Cover for
Deadpool #27
(April 2017). Art
by David Lopez.

RIGHT:
At your service!
Deadpool #27
(November
2010). Script
by Daniel
Way. Art by
Carlo Barberi
(pencils),
Walden Wong
(inks), Marte
Gracia (colors),
Joe Sabino
(letters).

I GREW UP IDOLIZING CAPTAIN AMERICA.

I FOUGHT HIM WHEN WE FIRST MET BECAUSE I WAS TOO NERVOUS TO TELL HIM WHAT A FAN I WAS.

IT'S BAD BUSINESS TO MEET YOUR HEROES, SO I TRIED TO KILL MINE.

THEN HE MADE ME AN AVENGER. IT WAS ONE OF THE WEIRDEST AND BEST DAYS OF MY LIFE.

NOT LONG AGO, HE HELPED ME STAY SANE THROUGH THE WORST THING I'D EVER BEEN THROUGH.

I NEED YOU TO FILL THE VOID THAT LOGAN LEFT BEHIND.

THERE'S A JOKE THERE SOMEWHERE, BUT SERIOUSLY-- THANK YOU.

LEFT: Hey, it was all Evil Deadpool's fault! *Deadpool #47* (February 2012). Script by Daniel Way. Art by Salva Espin (pencils, inks), Guru-eFX (colors), Joe Sabino (letters).

One is American, the other is Canadian. One is a world-famous Super Hero, the other is famous for being an untrustworthy mercenary. One wears a shield, the other weilds a pair of swords. But something unites the two: they were both transformed by disturbing government experiments!

That might be why Captain America—despite everything—has a certain respect for Deadpool and has given him several shots at redemption. Almost everybody knows about the experiment that turned a puny but brave boy from Brooklyn called Steve Rogers into the Super Soldier and heroic icon Captain America. Steve subjected himself voluntarily to an experiment that upgraded his strength, endurance, and agility to superhuman levels. These powers, combined with his strategic skill and deep sense of justice, made him an extraordinary fighter who could hold his own against individuals much more powerful than he was. Believed to have died in World War Two, Cap resurfaced years later, and since then he's been fighting on the front lines against evil.

The first encounter between the Living Legend and Wade Wilson goes all the way back to World War Two! Accompanied by Hydra Bob, Deadpool ended up going back in time by mistake and fought Baron Zemo alongside Cap and Bucky. Weasel's attempts to get them back to the present created temporal paradoxes, and Cap and Bucky forgot who Bob and Deadpool were and ended up attacking them!

Back in the present, Cap gave Wade a lot of chances, but even he eventually started to lose his patience. When the showdown between Deadpool and Evil Deadpool left a wake of destruction across New York City and New Jersey, Cap stepped in to stop Wade, not believing the "evil twin" excuse. Evil Deadpool himself proved his existence to Steve Rogers by assulating him!

In the following years, the leader of the Avengers took a personal interest in Wade Wilson, convinced that there was some good in him. The two of them, together with Wolverine, were also part of a tragic mission in North Korea where they discovered the painful shadows of his past, in the saga 'The Good, the Bad, and the Ugly.' Later on, when Wolverine was (temporarily) dead, Steve and Wade joined forces against A.I.M, to stop anyone from cloning Logan's body using traces of his DNA.

ABOVE:
Cover for *Deadpool #47* (February 2012). Art by Nick Bradshaw & Frank Martin Jr.

RIGHT:
Cover for *Deadpool #17* (November 2013). Art by Declan Shalvey & Jordie Bellaire.

But the greatest test of faith was when Steve Rogers recruited Wade Wilson for the Avengers Unity Squad, the team created to demonstrate cooperation between humans and mutants after the events of the *Avengers vs X-Men* series. Wade was part of the team, fighting alongside many other heroes and proving he knew how to be generous and altruistic, until Steve Rogers himself betrayed him. A corrupted doppleganger of Cap was created by the Cosmic Cube and he became a Hydra sleeper agent, ready to take control of the USA. When that happened, Deadpool followed Captain America blindly, going so far as to kill S.H.I.E.L.D. agent Phil Coulson, who had discovered Steve's secret plan. Since then, even after the return of the "real" Cap, Wade has started on a downward spiral that has distanced him from the good guys. Who knows whether Steve will be able to save Wade from himself again in the future… and whether Deadpool will go back to being Cap's trusted ally!

"When Rogers invited me onto his Avengers Unity Squad, I was taking Wolverine's roster spot. I knew why I was around. There were going to be tasks that other Avengers wouldn't be down for."

DEADPOOL

ABOVE: Trust issues, *Deadpool #27* (November 2010). Script by Daniel Way. Art by Carlo Barberi (pencils), Walden Wong (inks), Marte Gracia (colors), Joe Sabino (letters).

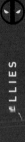

UNCANNY AVENGERS

Deadpool was an Avenger, too... but that didn't last long!

I t sounds unbelievable, but the "Earth's Mightiest Heroes" once counted Deadpool among their members! Wade was part of a specific team, the Avengers Unity Division. It was created after the events of the *Avengers vs X-Men* series, where the two groups were fighting for control of the Phoenix Force. At the end of the series, Cyclops was possessed by the Phoenix Force and it forced him to murder Professor Xavier. Soon after that, Captain America decided to actively support Xavier's dream of a world where humans and mutants could coexist. So, he founded a team that included members of both the X-Men and the Avengers, such as Wolverine, Rogue, Scarlet Witch, and Wonder Man.

After a few years, Cap offered a place on the team to Deadpool, having noticed the ex-merc's attempts at redemption. Besides, at the time D-Pool had practically become a billionaire, acquired his own base and even found time to have a brief romance with Rogue. Unfortunately, Wade's adventures with the Avengers came to an end when the Hydra-corrupted Steve Rogers recruited him for his nefarious schemes at the beginning of the *Secret Empire* event!

ABOVE:
Cover for *Uncanny Avengers #1* (December 2015). Art by Ryan Stegman & Richard Isanove.

RIGHT:
Deadpool isn't very good at teamwork. *Uncanny Avengers #1* (December 2015). Script by Gerry Duggan. Art by Ryan Stegman (pencils, inks), Richard Isanove (colors), Clayton Cowles.

OPPOSITE PAGE:
Deadpool leads the charge. *Uncanny Avengers #1* (December 2015). Script by Gerry Duggan. Art by Ryan Stegman (pencils, inks), Richard Isanove (colors), Clayton Cowles (letters).

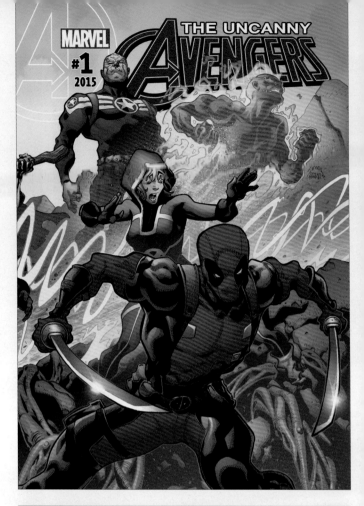

WOLVERINE

The most famous mutant was Wade's friend, enemy and compatriot.

Wolverine needs no introduction. Even those who know little about Super Heroes know about this Canadian mutant, who has three Adamantium claws on each hand, superhuman senses, and a healing factor that lets him patch up any wound and grants him a greatly increased lifespan.

The man called Logan has lived for more than a century, during which time he's been a soldier, a samurai, a secret agent, and a Super Hero. Logan was also a lab rat in a cruel experiment.In an attempt to make another perfect Super Soldier after Captain America, the Weapon X Program kidnapped him, his healing factor making him the perfect test subject for the excruciating experiments. Logan's skeleton, including his six retractable claws, were bound to an indestructible metal called Adamantium. The suffering he went through during the experiment reduced Logan to an almost animal state, as shown in the series *Weapon X*, written and drawn by Barry Windsor-Smith.

After his escape from the Weapon X Facility, it took years for Logan to regain control of his human nature again, and even longer for him to become a hero. Constantly fighting the feral fury inside him and determined to redeem himself for the violence he caused in the past, Wolverine has fought in the ranks of the X-Men for many years. He has also been an Avenger, and over the years he has taken many young mutants under his wing, becoming a gruff but reliable mentor.

RIGHT:
Wolverine versus Deadpool. *Wolverine #88* (December 1994). Script by Larry Hama. Art by Fabio Laguna (pencils), Tim Townsend (inks), Marie Javins (colors), Pat Brosseau (letters).

Logan's memories have been manipulated in a similar way to what happened to Deadpool, but the two of them have an even deeper bond, and no, it's not because they're both Canadian! When the Weapon X Program was dissolved, some of the results from its experiments survived… including the secret of Logan's healing factor. Years later, Department K, a secret Canadian organization, recruited Wade Wilson in order to perform an experiment similar to the one that had turned Logan into the perfect killing machine. The scientists of Department K cured Wade's cancer by injecting Logan's mutant power into his body. Essentially, Deadpool's biggest advantage exists thanks to the famous mutant!

Their first official encounter —in *Wolverine* #88 (December 1994)—saw Wolvie rescue Garrison Kane and Vanessa. At the time, Logan and Wade's ex-girlfriend Vanessa were living together and trying to build a new life in San Francisco. Deadpool attacked them, determined to get Vanessa back at any cost, but unfortunately

ABOVE:
Cover for
Wolverine #88
(December
1994). Art by
Adam Kubert

LEFT:
Wade Wilson
fights alongside
Wolverine and
X-Force. *Fear
Itself: Uncanny
X-Force #2*
(October 2011).
Script by Rob
Williams. Art by
Simone Bianchi
(pencils, inks),
Simone Peruzzi
(colors), Joe
Sabino (letters).

for him Logan had just arrived to protect Kane, sent by a mutual friend, James Hudson. This skirmish, which ended with Deadpool on the run, was the first in a long line of battles between the two Canadians. Wolverine and Deadpool have fought on several occasions and there hasn't always been a clear winner.

Over the years, though, as Deadpool attempted to redeem himself by fighting more often on the good guys' side (or at least by choosing which cause to unsheathe his katanas for more carefully), Wolverine tried to give him a chance. Lately, Wolverine and Deadpool have stopped attacking

each other and fought side by side instead. They also teamed up in X-Force, the mutant black ops team captained by Wolvie and in which Wade has often played a crucial role. Today, Logan is one of the few people who can really understand Deadpool… and one of the few who can stop him.

*"You're Wolverine, the berserker wildman of the woods.
You're the best at what you do and what you do isn't pretty.
Now, that means you kill people, right? Right? That's you."*

DEADPOOL

VANESSA

Also know as Copycat, she was Deadpool's first true love.
It was the beginning of a star-crossed tragedy.

A prostitute and a mercenary might not seem like the perfect couple, but at least Vanessa Carlysle and Wade Wilson were happy. Unfortunately, when Wade found out he had a tumor, he decided to leave Vanessa so she wouldn't have to suffer. No one could have predicted that Wade would go on to become Deadpool! Later on, Vanessa, who is a shape-shifting mutant, also became a mercenary, with the code name Copycat. She was recruited by the evil Tolliver, who convinced her to to impersonate Domino and spy on Cable as a member of X-Force.

For a year, Domino was Tolliver's prisoner, until Copycat eventually decided to rebel against the evil mutant, before vanishing when Domino was freed. Later on, Vanessa was recruited for the new version of the Weapon X project, but the "upgrades" she endured tampered with her memory and her mental stability. She was deemed unreliable and Weapon X hired none other than Deadpool, one of the program's recruits at the time, to assassinate her. Instead he fell in love and pledged to protect her. In the end, Weapon X sent the cyborg Garrison Kane and Sabretooth to kill her—gutted by Sabretooth, the mutant died in Wade's arms.

LEFT:
Years later, Vanessa keeps an eye on Wade... but wasn't she dead?! From *Deadpool #27* (April 2014). Script by Fabian Nicieza. Art by Scott Hepburn (pencils, inks), Val Staples (colors) & Joe Sabino (letters).

OPPOSITE PAGE BOTTOM:
Cover for *X-Force #7* (September 2014). Art by Rock-He Kim.

OPPOSITE PAGE:
Cover for *Deadpool & the Mercs for Money #1* (September 2016). Art by Iban Coello & Nolan Woodard.

"Vanessa! Copycat! I haven't seen you in a while... outside of the movies!"

DEADPOOL

DOMINO

This lucky mutant was unlucky enough to meet Deadpool.

Neena Thurman, aka Domino, is a mutant with a truly bizarre power: she can subconsciously manipulate her surroundings so that the odds are always in her favor. In short, she's pretty darn lucky. Someone fighting Domino might find themselves with a misfiring pistol, or a piano could suddenly fall on their head. For her part, Neena could survive by falling off a rooftop onto a truck piled high with mattresses, or guess a security code on the first try.

But there was one time when her luck wasn't enough: years ago, at the beginning of the first *X-Force* series, the evil Tolliver kidnapped her to replace her with Vanessa. Tolliver used the shape-shifting mutant to spy on his enemy Cable. At the time, Tolliver had hired Deadpool as his henchman, and when Cable came to Domino's aid, the two of them came up against the Merc with a Mouth himself!

In the years after that, Domino and Deadpool have had various face-offs, but also ended up collaborating. A while back, Neena formed a new team, Mercs for Money, taking control of a group that had originally been founded and led by Deadpool. Over the years the two of them have been both allies and enemies. There's a close bond between them, built on mutual (though well-hidden) respect, and cemented by the various battles they've fought side-by-side—along with the shared experience of both being victims of painful experiments.

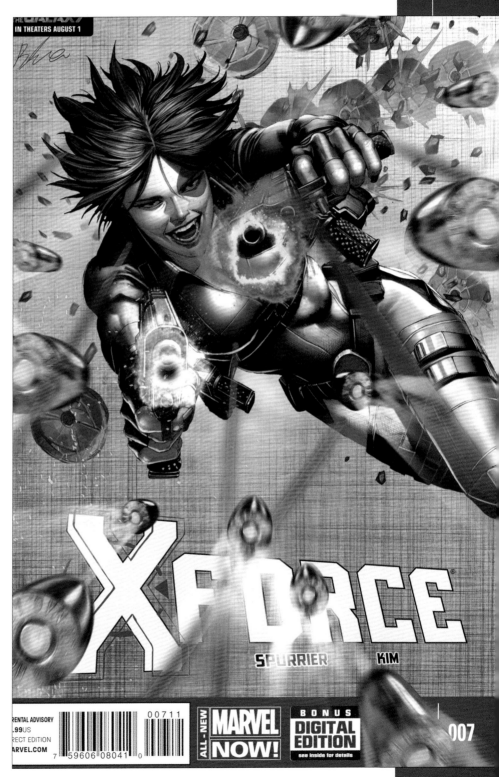

LADY DEADPOOL

She was the female version of the Merc with a Mouth who sacrificed her life to save the Deadpool Corps.

Lady Deadpool is the Merc with a Mouth's female counterpart. Her name is Wanda Wilson, and she comes from Earth-3010, an alternate reality where she's the head of rebels fighting a repressive American government.

She and Deadpool met for the first time in *Deadpool: Merc with a Mouth #7* (2010), in a short story written by Victor Gischler and drawn by Rob Liefeld. They fought side by side against General America, the anti-democratic Captain America of that world and the Merc with a Mouth quickly fell in love with his new ally. But Wanda was already in love with rebel leader Charles Fey, an ex-actor and former bodyguard, who had been captured by the authorities while working on a revolutionary campaign. Lady Deadpool managed to free him, but Fey died during the attempted escape.

Lady Deadpool became leader of the Deadpool Corps, a team of Deadpools from alternate universes, with whom she fought Dreadpool, another alternate (and darker) version of the Merc from Earth-12101. Unfortunately, her story ended tragically in *Deadpool Kills Deadpool #3*: to save her comrades, Wanda drove the spaceship *Bea Arthur* into Galactipool, heroically sacrificing herself.

RIGHT:
Lady Deadpool encounters General America in *Deadpool: Merc with a Mouth #7*. Script by Victor Gischler. Art by Rob Liefeld (pencils, inks, colors), Jeff Eckleberry (letters).

BOTTOM RIGHT:
To kill or not to kill? From *Deadpool Kills Deadpool #3* (November 2013). Script by Cullen Bunn. Art by Salva Espin (pencils, inks), Veronica Gandini (colors), Joe Sabino (letters).

SIRYN

An Irish mutant who tried to save Deadpool from himself.

S he's a mutant, she's Irish, and she's got an earsplitting power. Theresa Rourke Cassidy, aka Siryn, is the daughter of Sean Cassidy, aka Banshee, former member of the X-Men and ex-Interpol agent. Theresa was unaware of her origins for a long time. When she was still a baby, her mother was tragically killed by an IRA bomb while her father was on an undercover mission. Her uncle Black Tom, Banshee's evil brother, adopted Theresa and hid her from her real father for decades.

One of Theresa's most famous adventures was *Deadpool: Sins of the Past*, which you'll read about in the following pages. In this limited series, she teamed up with Deadpool and confronted Black Tom and his longtime ally, the unstoppable, superstrong Juggernaut. This was also the beginning of a spark between the two, despite the fact they'd known each other for a while. Deadpool had become a thorn in the side of X-Force, the team Siryn was a member of at the time, but his attraction to her began to calm him down a little. Siryn also slowly began to feel attracted to Wade, despite his appearance, bad reputation, and Sean and Cable's warnings. Later on, Siryn and Deadpool had many adventures together, especially when Wade crossed paths with X-Force, as well as sporadic moments of passion.

"Oooh that man! I can never tell if he's serious or not! Deadpool! Come back here! I'm nae joking!"

SIRYN

LEFT:
Siryn rescues Wade. *Deadpool #1* (August 1994). Script by Mark Waid. Art by Ian Churchill (pencils), Jason Temujin Minor (inks), Dana Moreshead (colors), Richard Starkings (letters).

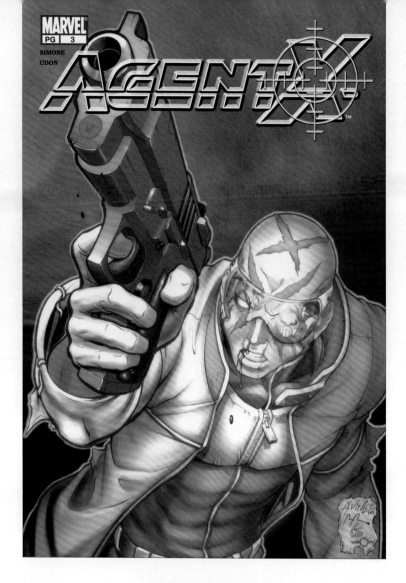

AGENT X

The mystery of Alex Hayden! Who was Agent X? Was he really Deadpool?

Years ago, Deadpool ended up as the head of a successful mercenary agency, D.P. Inc, managed by the trusty Sandi Brandenberg. An assignment saw him hired by one of the Four Winds, a Japanese criminal organization, to settle an internal dispute between the bosses. Wade got credit for killing all the bosses, which enraged Black Swan, a mutant mercenary. Black Swan hired Nijo, the brother of one of the criminals supposedly killed by Wade, to get revenge. Nijo started to spy on Wade, who was becoming weaker and weaker because of a "mental virus" that Black Swan had infected him with. However, Nijo soon realized that Black Swan was a dishonorable villain who was hiding something.

Later on Wade confronted Black Swan in his castle in Germany, and the mutant revealed that he was actually the one who killed the Four Winds. Nijo had now switched sides, and with his help Wade faced Black Swan, but the encounter was interrupted by the detonation of a bomb that Deadpool had hidden in the castle, which seemingly killed the trio. A while later, a guy with incredible combat skills and strange scars on his face showed up at Sandi's door. She was convinced it was Wade. As he had lost his memory, she renamed him Alex Hayden. Alex, determined to become the best mercenary ever, started a new agency, Agency X, with the mutant Outlaw and Taskmaster, a longtime enemy of the Avengers who was able to imitate others' abilities. Alex Hayden had many adventures, recounted in the sixteen issues of the series *Agent X*, which replaced the *Deadpool* series.

In the grand finale, the real Deadpool reappeared… along with Black Swan. The latter revealed that in the explosion he'd used his mental gifts to link himself to Wade and Nijo, uniting their powers, memories, and personalities. Black Swan had survived by stealing Deadpool's powers and Alex Hayden was just Nijo's body… resuscitated by Wade's healing factor and equipped with Black Swan's abilities! Alex/Nijo, Wade, and their allies defeated Black Swan, and since then Agent X has embarked upon new adventures, still in search of his own identity.

RIGHT:
Cover for *Agent X #3* (November 2002). Art by Udon Studios.

AGENT OF HYDRA

He was an ordinary henchman,
working for an extraordinary antihero.

Hydra is one of the oldest, most feared terrorist organizations in the Marvel Universe. It has tons of members, small cogs in a huge machine where only the top leaders like Viper, Baron Zemo, and Arnim Zola are known.

One of the many ordinary people who have joined Hydra, more out of convenience than ideology, was a guy named Bob. He joined the organization to show his wife he was capable of doing something… and for the corporate benefits! Unfortunately for him, he was in Deadpool's way when the mutant infiltrated a Hydra facility to free his ally Alex Hayden, Agent X. Wade convinced Bob (the hard way) to help him out. Since then, Bob has often been forced by Deadpool to give him a hand on increasingly crazy and dangerous missions — whether it's among dinosaurs in the Savage Land, or on risky journeys through time. This was despite the fact that the ex-henchman didn't have any superpowers or special abilities… except running away when he was in danger!

LEFT:
Poor, poor Bob… *Cable & Deadpool #38* (May 2007). Script by Fabian Nicieza. Art by Reilly Brown (pencils), Pat Davidson & Jeremy Freeman (inks), Gotham (colors), Dave Sharpe (letters).

---

*"Plan Z…? What're the odds even he would screw up
twenty-five other possibilities?"*

BOB

DEADPOOL'S OTHER ALLIES

Villains, secret agents, arms dealers, Super Heroes… and more Deadpools.

ABOVE:
With friends like these…
Cable & Deadpool #36 (March 2007). Script by Fabian Nicieza. Art by Reilly Brown (pencils), Jeremy Freeman (inks), Gotham (colors), Dave Sharpe (letters).

Given his temper, it's not easy for Deadpool to make friends, but a lot of people have fought at his side (more or less voluntarily) over the years! One of the oldest is Jack Hammer, aka Weasel. Weasel decided to get into crime after running into Wade by chance and became his assistant and arms dealer. Later on, he was killed by one of Deadpool's enemies and came back to life as the evil Patient Zero, thanks to a deal with Mephisto.

Another of the mercenary's old friends is Blind Al, an old woman with a mysterious past. Possibly a former spy, she met Wade when he was hired to kill her. Instead he spared her and they became friends.

Emily Preston, agent of S.H.I.E.L.D., was told to recruit Wade to stop an invasion of zombie presidents. She was killed by an undead George Washington, but her consciousness was first put inside Wade's mind, then into an LMD (Life Model Decoy) robot with her features. She became an important ally of Wade's — after a while the mercenary even left her with his newfound daughter, Eleanor. And of course someone as crazy as Deadpool needs a crazy friend like Typhoid Mary, Daredevil's old enemy

(and ex-lover). A woman with multiple personalities, she's also Mary Walker and Bloody Mary—and each of them has different goals from the others.

Other disreputable ladies include (the name says it all) the B.A.D. Girls, a group of three very dangerous young women — Asp, Black Mamba, and Diamondback — who originally fought the Merc and later became his allies. Another frenemy was Outlaw, created by Gail Simone and Udon Studios and appearing in *Deadpool #65*, A mercenary who's super-skilled with weapons, she had a fling with Deadpool, who also saved her from T-Ray after he kidnapped her.

No one could forget monster hunter Elsa Bloodstone, Deadpool's latest flame, daughter of Ulysses Bloodstone, and a member of Nextwave, Midnight Sons, and the Fearless Defenders. Other more recent acquaintances include the mutant Negasonic Teenage Warhead, who was Deadpool's latest assistant and who loves making fun of him. There's also power-stealing mutant Rogue, who fought at Wade's side in the Uncanny Avengers—for a while there was something between them, too. Gwenpool has a similar look and name to our Merc; for a while it was thought that she came from your reality, but it was later revealed that she's a mutant. Finally, speaking of allies, how could we forget the Deadpool Corps? After all, who could be a better friend than all the alternate versions of yourself from parallel worlds?

TOLLIVER

An arms trader who came from the future
to get revenge on Cable, using Deadpool and Copycat.

His name is Tolliver—or Mr. Tolliver—as he likes to be called. But maybe we should say Tyler Dayspring. Or Genesis. Are you confused? So are we…

Tolliver first appeared in *X-Force* in 1991, a brainchild of Deadpool's creators (Rob Liefeld and Fabian Nicieza). He made a violent entrance into the Merc with a Mouth's world when he kidnapped the mutant Domino, as revealed in *X-Force #11*. His goal was to have Copycat/Vanessa replace Domino and infiltrate X-Force. He failed. In a battle with Cable, Tolliver's helicopter exploded and it looked as if he'd died. But that's not what actually happened. Tolliver would return, mysterious as ever, but in the meantime, the mercenaries competed with each other to inherit his weapons and maps.

Born in the alternate future of Earth-4935, the Super Villain called Tyler was really the son of the mutant Cable (Nathan Dayspring) and Aliya, who was killed when the young mutant was kidnapped and brainwashed by Cable's evil clone Stryfe. Later on, Tyler introduced himself to his father as one of Stryfe's soldiers—Cable, not recognising his son, shot him to save his friend Dawnsilk, who had been taken hostage. Tyler decided to travel into the past to get revenge on Cable, assuming the alias of Mr. Tolliver, a ruthless arms dealer.

His latest alias was Genesis, leader of the Dark Riders, a fanatical group devoted to Darwinian ideals, and self-proclaimed successor to Apocalypse, the first mutant on Earth and X-Men Super Villain.

*"You're Nathan, right? I'm Deadpool.
Pleased to meet you. Mr. Tolliver hired me to find you."*

DEADPOOL

NORMAN OSBORN

The Merc saved his life by traveling back in time, but Osborn was anything but grateful...

When Green Goblin threw Gwen Stacy off the Brooklyn Bridge in *Amazing Spider-Man #121,* leading to her death, many readers shed real tears. They hated the cold-blooded murderer who killed Peter Parker's girlfriend. In his unique green and purple suit, Green Goblin is the archenemy of Spider-Man and completely obsessed with his foe. And since Deadpool is supposed to be "Spider-Man, except with guns and swords, a jackass," as Rob Liefeld described him, of course their paths were going to cross.

His real name is Norman Osborn, a rich widowed businessman, and father to Harry, Peter's classmate. In order to use a power-enhancing serum on himself, Osborn has its creator Mendel Stromm arrested, but the experiment goes badly wrong. Osborn becomes stronger. But the experiment

fails: Osborn becomes stronger, but the formula's side-effects drive him insane.

Osborn's first encounter with Deadpool took place in *Deadpool #11.* Traveling back in time with Blind Al, Deadpool found himself at the time of the events of *Amazing Spider-Man #47,* and even managed to save Norman's life! Not out of the goodness of his heart, but because he had taken Spider-Man's place and didn't want to alter the timeline. It was not the start

of a friendship. In fact, during their next encounter decades later, Norman played a dirty trick on Deadpool when he intercepted the Skrull data that the latter had stolen, making him lose out on a big reward. Osborn was also one of the protagonists of the story arcs 'One of Us' and 'Magnum Opus.'

It's been an ongoing rivalry. To get rid of Deadpool, Osborn has sent the likes of Tiger Shark and Bob to kill him, as well as the Thunderbolts and Bullseye, but always without success.

Moreover, during this comedy of errors, Deadpool almost accidentally helped his enemy when he decided to kill Ellis Kincaid, a man who wrongly accused the X-Men of keeping his daughter hostage. If he had gone through with it, he would have played right into Norman Osborn's hands, as the latter wanted to frame the mutants for Kincaid's murder, making them the villains in the story. Luckily, in the end Kincaid revealed that Osborn was behind the whole thing.

"Please, Al, a little warning next time... Some of us aren't blind, y'know?"

DEADPOOL

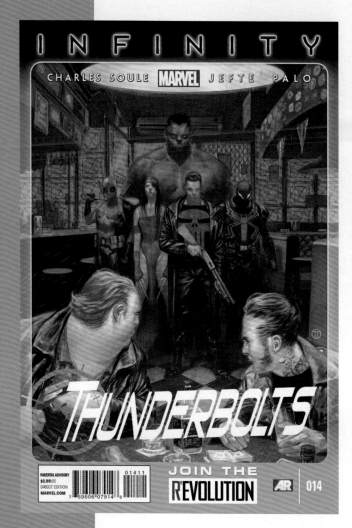

THUNDERBOLTS

Meet the strange group of Super Villains disguised as Super Heroes —which naturally included Deadpool at one point.

ABOVE:
Cover from
Thunderbolts
#14 (October
2013). Art by
Julian Totino
Tedesco.

RIGHT:
Cover from
Thunderbolts
#19 (February
2014). Art by
Julian Totino
Tedesco.

All the Super Heroes had disappeared, apparently dead after the arrival of Onslaught—a psionic entity created from the consciousness of the world's two strongest mutants, Professor Charles Xavier, leader of the X-Men, and his archenemy Magneto. In reality, they were transported to an alternate universe created by Franklin Richards (son of Reed and Sue Richards), hidden away from the world. With all the heroes gone, Baron Zemo had an ingenious idea: create a new super team that he controlled,

made up of villains with less than noble goals.

And so several "bad guys" got together. The Beetle became Mach-1, Goliath was Atlas, Moonstone was called Meteorite, Screaming Mimi was Songbird, and Fixer was Techno. Last but not least, Zemo renamed himself Citizen V. Together, they were the Thunderbolts, a team created by Kurt Busiek and featured in Peter David and Mike Deodato Jr.'s *The Incredible Hulk #449* (1997).

It was a gripping series, full of twists and turns, with protagonists

who were always toeing the dangerous, fascinating line between good and evil. After the 'Civil War' crossover, the line-up of the group changed. The new Thunderbolts members were Norman Osborn, Moonstone, Songbird, Venom, Radioactive Man, Swordsman, Bullseye, and Penance. Deadpool has regularly run into them since 2008 (see the crossover *Dark Reign*), even becoming a member of the Red Hulk's Thunderbolts, along with Elektra, Agent Venom, and Punisher in Marvel NOW!

VILLAINS

"WHAT DOES THAT WORD EVEN *MEAN*?"

ABOVE:
Cover from *Thunderbolts* *#131* (June 2009). Art by Francesco Mattina.

FAR LEFT:
The incredible *Red* Hulk from *Thunderbolts* *#8* (June 2013). Script by Daniel Way Art by Phil Noto (pencils, inks), Guru-eFX (colors), Joe Sabino (letters).

LEFT:
The beautiful Black Widow in "Magnum Opus Part 3: Hard to Get". *Deadpool* *#9* (June 2009). Script by Daniel Way. Art by Paco Medina (pencils), Juan Vlasco (inks), Marte Gracia (colors), Cory Petit (letters).

67

MADCAP

He is the immortal being who became one with Deadpool.

Madcap knows Deadpool well… because he has lived inside him! But let's not get ahead of ourselves. Years ago, the man who would become Madcap set off on a religious field trip with other believers, but their bus was mistakenly blown up by A.I.M., the terrorists intending to destroy the chemical Compound X07, which could heal any wound. The man, whose real name is unknown, survived and lay in a puddle of the compound for hours. After regaining consciousness and discovering he was the sole survivor, he attempted to kill himself in despair, only to find out he was invincible.

Now doubting there was any rational meaning behind his existence, Madcap's mission became to drive people insane. After encounters with various heroes like Daredevil and She-Hulk, he challenged Deadpool, which in turn led to a fight with Thor, as revealed in *Deadpool Annual #1*, vol. 3 (2013). Thor struck the two of them with a lightning bolt, but when they regenerated, Madcap ended up in Wade's mind! He stayed there for a few years, popping up in his thoughts (the white boxes with black text) until they were separated. He came back later on other occasions: once he impersonated Deadpool and killed innocent people, and another time he bonded to Bob, Agent of Hydra, as a parasite!

RIGHT:
The moment where everything changed. *Deadpool Annual #1* (January 2014). Script by Ben Acker & Ben Blacker. Art by Evan "Doc" Shaner (pencils, inks), Veronica Gandini (colors), Joe Sabino (letters).

OPPOSITE PAGE:
Two minds become one. *Deadpool Annual #1* (January 2014). Script by Ben Acker & Ben Blacker. Art by Evan "Doc" Shaner (pencils, inks), Veronica Gandini (colors), Joe Sabino (letters).

SABRETOOTH

As if his own enemies weren't enough, the Merc with a Mouth almost stole Logan's archenemy!

Even though everyone considers Victor "Sabretooth" Creed to be Wolverine's archenemy, his life and Wade Wilson's are deeply entangled.

Although we don't know much about Creed's past, we do know he was born over a hundred years ago. Since childhood, he's had pointy teeth, razor-sharp claws, and homicidal instincts. Chained up in a basement by his parents, he managed to get free by biting off his own hand and then exacted revenge on his father. From that time on, he started traveling around America, often crossing paths with Logan, who would later become Wolverine.

Years later, Sabretooth ended up being a lab rat in one of the first versions of the Weapon X project, the same program that would experiment on Logan and Wade. It isn't yet clear what Victor got out of those experiments, aside from huge gaps in his memory. In the years after that, Creed was a ruthless mercenary and secret agent, and later on he started working for Mister Sinister. The latter, a cloning expert, cloned Victor many times—often when Sabretooth was assumed dead, it was actually one of his clones!

Later on, Creed was recruited for a new version of the Weapon X Project. The program infused his bones and claws with Adamantium, just as had been done to Logan years earlier. Now even more lethal, Sabretooth actually wanted to spy on the new Weapon X Project and its director's activities and then run away. Biding his time before betraying the group, he carried out various missions for them. One of these consisted of recruiting Deadpool in the 2001 series *Agent of Weapon X*. One of Deadpool's first missions on the team was to eliminate a former agent, and his ex-girlfriend: Vanessa, aka Copycat. Wade refused and decided to help her

instead, but Sabretooth killed her—déjà-vu again for anyone who's familiar with Victor and Logan's encounters!

Years later, Creed fought Wade again, but this time, the situation was a little different. A spell had reversed Sabretooth's morals, turning him into one of the good guys, and he even fought briefly for the Uncanny Avengers and the X-Men. Wade pursued him after

finding out he was the one who killed his parents. But Deadpool's memory, just like Sabretooth's, had been greatly modified: it was actually Wade who had killed his own parents. It happened on a mission that his old "employer," Butler, had manipulated him into taking on. Sabretooth was there, but the one who set fire to their house was Wade!

MARVEL COMICS
DEADPOOL: AGENT OF WEAPON X

MARVEL PG #2 58

TIERI   JEANTY   HOLDREDGE

SHIKLAH

The queen of the monsters, who fell in love with Deadpool!

Before humans came to be, Shiklah and her family ruled the monster realm. But their race ended up at war with the Vampires… and lost! Locked away in a sarcophagus, the beautiful warrior Shiklah could transform into a terrible monster.. Thousands of years later, Dracula hired Deadpool to recover the sarcophagus so he could marry the Queen, legitimizing his rule over the monsters. But Shiklah ended up falling in love with Wade… and they got married instead!

The wedding was officiated by Nightcrawler, and there were many X-Men and Avengers among the guests. The cover of *Deadpool #27* even made the Guinness World Records because of the huge number of characters drawn by Scott Koblish! Deadpool and Shiklah went on to become the rulers of the underground Monster Metropolis.

Later on, though, as Deadpool got busier and busier on heroic missions in the

ABOVE: Introducing husband and wife. *Deadpool #27* (June 2014). Script by Brian Posehn & Gerry Duggan. Art by Mike Hawthorne (pencils, inks), Jordie Bellaire (colors), Joe Sabino (letters).

ABOVE RIGHT: Trouble in paradise. *Deadpool #44* (May 2015). Script by Brian Posehn & Gerry Duggan. Art by Salva Espin (pencils, inks), Val Staples (colors), Joe Sabino (letters). *Fantastic Four #560* (November 2008). Art by Bryan Hitch.

RIGHT: The "smile" of the Queen, *Deadpool #44* (May 2015). Script by Brian Posehn & Gerry Duggan. Art by Salva Espin (pencils, inks), Val Staples (colors), Joe Sabino (letters).

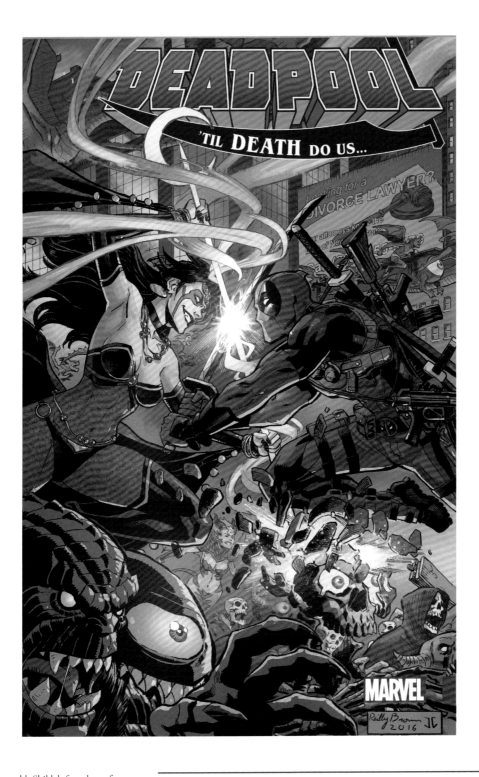

surface world, Shiklah found comfort in other creatures. Though Shiklah cheated on him, Deadpool seemed not to notice, and his negligence fueled the queen's rage. When one of her subjects was killed by humans, Shiklah finally declared war on Manhattan and her villainous side emerged unchecked. Deadpool chose to defend the humans and asked for Dracula's help to do it. Once the battle was over, Dracula married Shiklah… annulling her marriage with Wade!

"I don't get too many happy endings. That's not a euphemismmph! For one night, everything in the world was perfect…"

DEADPOOL

EVIL DEADPOOL

All the worst parts of the original Deadpool, put together!

Between battles, explosions, and duels, Deadpool has lost pieces of himself all over the world. Arms, legs, feet, toes… and some of those pieces were collected by Dr. Ella Whitby, a crazy British scientist who was obsessed with Deadpool! After the lovesick doctor tried to kill him, he gathered up the limbs to dispose of them, chucking them into the garbage. Unfortunately those body parts also had his healing factor. They joined together, creating a deformed, monstrous body—a sort of twisted reflection of Wade Wilson… Evil Deadpool!

The two of them fought for the first time when Evil Deadpool blew up Wade's favorite chimichanga joint. Determined to replace the real Deadpool, Evil Deadpool has returned several times, even after appearing to have been totally defeated. He was also one of the enemies recruited by the ex-Interpol agent Allison Kemp when she was trying to get revenge on Wade. On one occasion, Evil Deadpool allied with the Evil Deadpool Corps, a team of evil versions of Wade from different parallel worlds led by Dreadpool, the Deadpool from Earth-12101 and protagonist of the miniseries *Deadpool Kills the Marvel Universe*.

Evil Deadpool's powers are exactly the same as the real Deadpool's, including his amazing ability to come back to life. What makes him even more unpredictable is that his left arm is attached backwards!

RIGHT:
The truly twisted Evil Deadpool. Cover for *Deadpool #45* (December 2011). Script by Daniel Way. Art by Nick Bradshaw.

OPPOSITE PAGE:
Seeing double! *Deadpool #47* (February 2012). Script by Daniel Way. Art by Salva Espin (pencils, inks), Guru-eFX (colors), Joe Sabino (letters).

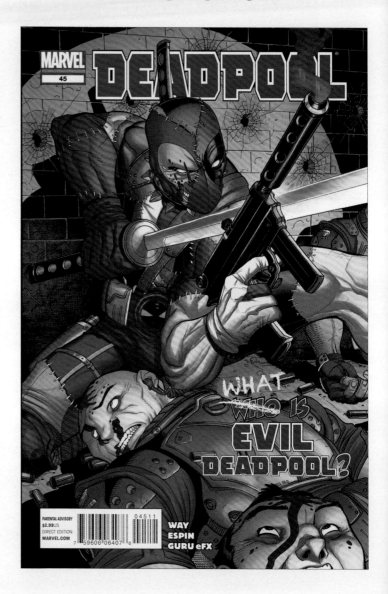

"It just became apparent to her that even if she killed you, sooner or later, you'd just come back. Y'know… like herpes. Or me."

EVIL DEADPOOL

ABOVE:
Ajax is back from the dead… for revenge. *Deadpool #17* (June 1998). Script by Joe Kelly. Art by Walter McDaniel (pencils), John Livesay (inks). Chris Sotomayor (colors), Richard Starkings & Comicraft (letters).

OPPOSITE PAGE:
Ajax vs Deadpool. *Deadpool #18* (July 1998). Script by Joe Kelly. Art by Walter McDaniel (pencils), John Livesay (inks). Chris Sotomayor (colors), Richard Starkings & Comicraft (letters).

AJAX

He is Deadpool's archenemy… who always comes back.

Francis is the assistant of Dr. Killebrew, the scientist who tortured the rejects from the Weapon X Project with bizarre experiments.

One victim of Killebrew's experiments was the guy who would become Deadpool, the only one of those locked in the Hospice who could resist Francis's provocations. Tired and jealous, Francis even tried to kill him, but in the meantime the healing factor, a result of the experiments that had been carried out on him, saved Wade. When he finally managed to escape the lab, Wade ended up running into Francis and shot him, but Killebrew saved his assistant. Operating on his former colleague, the Doctor transformed him into a super-powered cyborg, incapable of feeling pain. Several months before his origin story was revealed, the character first appeared in *Deadpool 14, vol. 3* (1998) under the codename of Ajax.

Soon after his transformation, Francis went off in search of Deadpool and the other survivors of the Weapon X Project. Many encounters later, Deadpool finally managed to kill Ajax, sending his systems into short circuit after breaking his neck and throwing him into a lake. Later on, though, Ajax came back to life thanks to a deal with the demon Blackheart—who had kidnapped death and sent both Deadpool and Thanos off in a search for their mutual love. Francis became Abyss Man, but he wasn't enough to stop Thanos and Deadpool. The combined forces of the Mad Titan and the Merc With a Mouth sent Francis back to his proper place in hell.

T-RAY

This ruthless killer for hire claimed he was the real Wade Wilson...
but who was he really?

T-Ray is a killer who tattoos the names of his intended victims on his back, crossing them out once he's killed them. He's a sadist, no doubt about it. T-Ray still hasn't managed to cross off the name "Wilson" on his skin, but maybe he will someday.

There isn't a Super Villain more ruthless, cruel, and immoral than this albino giant, who first appeared in *Deadpool #1*, vol. 1 (1997). He and Deadpool have also fought over their identity. It's a long story, one we already covered in the section on origins. We know that Jack, a runaway mercenary, was saved by Wade and Mercedes Wilson. To "thank" them for their generosity, Jack attacked Wade, stealing his identity, and killed Mercedes. But T-Ray swore that *he* was the real Wade Wilson.

Later on, T-Ray went to Japan, where he sold his soul to the Dark Masters in exchange for a new appearance, and after that he regularly showed up to kill Deadpool, always claiming there could only be one Wade Wilson.

RIGHT:
Cover from
Deadpool #33
(October 1999).
Art by Gus
Vazquez.

**OPPOSITE
PAGE:**
A big clash
between
Deadpool and
T-Ray. From
Deadpool #33
(October 1999),
"The End or Happy
Entrails to You."
Script by Joe
Kelly. Art by
David Brewer
(pencils),
Rodney Ramos
(inks), Shannon
Blanchard
(colors),
Richard
Starkings and
Comicraft
(letters).

"In T-Ray's mixed-up memories — ones that he shared with me — I was wearing my Deadpool costume when he found me. But I didn't become Deadpool until after I left Project X."

DEADPOOL

DEADPOOL'S MANY ENEMIES

A non-exhaustive list of people more dangerous than Deadpool.

After a lifetime spent fighting good guys and bad guys, Deadpool has a lot of enemies. Some, like Slayback, were from his past: the two of them were experimented on while part of the Weapon X project, with Slayback being given cyborg implants and a healing factor. Too dangerous and sociopathic even for Deadpool, Wade eventually decided to finish him off, but Slayback managed to survive and come back years later to get revenge.

During one of their confrontations, Slayback was recruited by Allison Kemp, ex-FBI and Interpol agent. Seriously injured by an explosive planted by Deadpool, Allison had devoted her life to stopping him. She studied Wade for years and was one of the few people who truly understood how the Merc's mind worked.

Another classic enemy was Black Swan, a German mutant mercenary who was capable of implanting a psionic virus into his enemies. He was eventually killed by the combined forces of Wade and Agent X.

This list wouldn't be complete without bizarre-looking enemies like Doctor Bong (a scientist with an enormous bell for a head) or the alien mercenary Macho Gomez. The former even put aside his criminal career for a while to become Deadpool's psychiatrist… until the two of them ended up fighting (with Steve Rogers and his Secret Avengers). Macho Gomez, for his part, was a mercenary who ended up competing with Deadpool, even on space missions!

ABOVE:
Not so nice… Slayback! From *Deadpool: The Circle Chase #3* (October 1993). Script by Fabian Nicieza. Art by Joe Madureira (pencils), Harry Candelario (inks), Glynis Oliver (colors), Chris Eliopoulos (letters).

RIGHT:
The first appearance of Black Swan in *Deadpool #65* (May 2002). Script by Gail Simone. Art by Udon Studios (pencils, inks, colors), David Sharpe (letters).

OPPOSITE PAGE:
Enter the Super Villain… Macho Gomez! *Deadpool #32* (March 2011). Script by Daniel Way. Art by Sheldon Vella (pencils, inks, colors), Joe Sabino (letters).

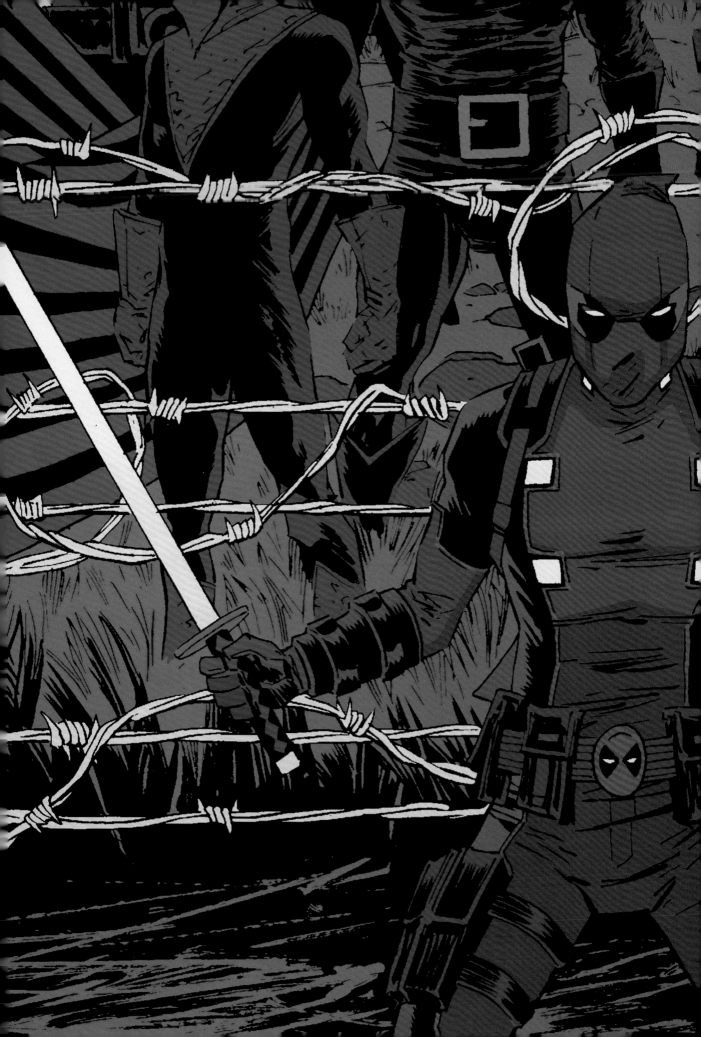

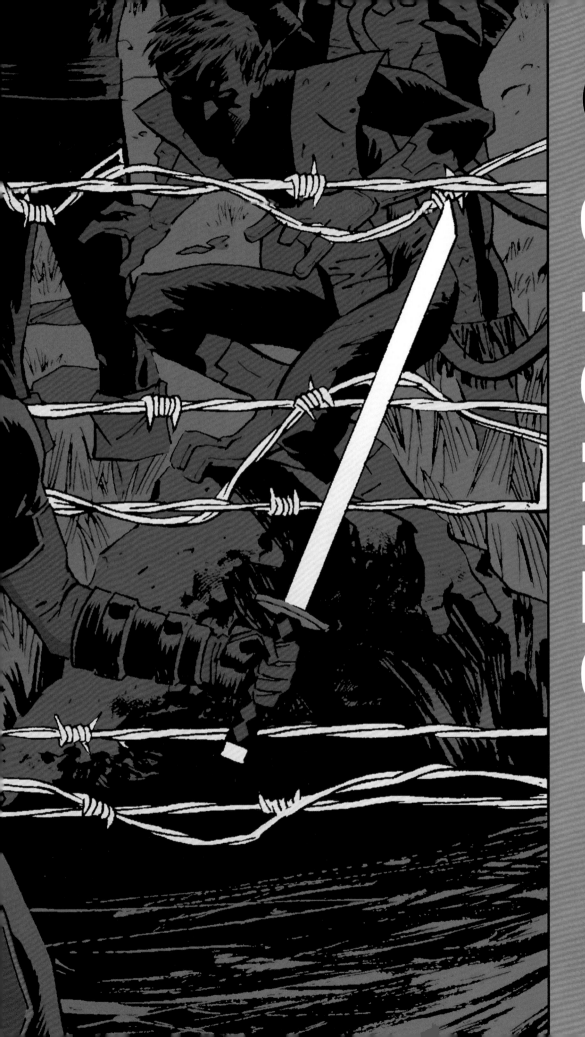

STORIES

THE CIRCLE CHASE

Deadpool searched for Vanessa across the world, only to find out she didn't love the Merc anymore...

What was Deadpool doing in Sarajevo, Egypt, and Nepal? After his guest appearances in *The New Mutants* and *X-Force*, the Merc with a Mouth finally got his first miniseries, *Deadpool: The Circle Chase*. It was 1993 (as you can probably tell from Joe Maureira's super-muscular style) and the readers had asked for Deadpool to be the protagonist, not merely a guest. Fabian Nicieza, his co-creator and author of

this three-chapter series, tied the story back to earlier events to start off this whirlwind around-the-world adventure.

The supposed death of Tolliver had sent the mercenary world into chaos as everyone hunted for the Super Villain's will, contained instruction on how to find his legendary stash of weapons. In Sarajevo, Deadpool ran into Weasel as well as Weapon X, who wanted information from him. Things were complicated by the fact that Nyko was

also there, and he was determined to avenge the death of his twin, Pico (one of Tolliver's henchmen). Enter Slayback, Black Tom and Juggernaut who chased Deadpool to Egypt as he hunted for Tolliver's fortune.

After being imprisoned in Sarajevo by the Executive Elite and then freed by Weasel, Deadpool headed to Nepal to find Vanessa. In the final showdown, the Merc With a Mouth saved his one true love from Slayback... only to find out she no longer loved him!

ABOVE: Deadpool makes a entrance on the scene. *Deadpool: The Circle Chase #1* (August 1993). Script by Fabian Nicieza. Art by Joe Madureira (pencils) Mark Farmer (inks), Glynis Oliver (colors), Chris Eliopoulos (letters).

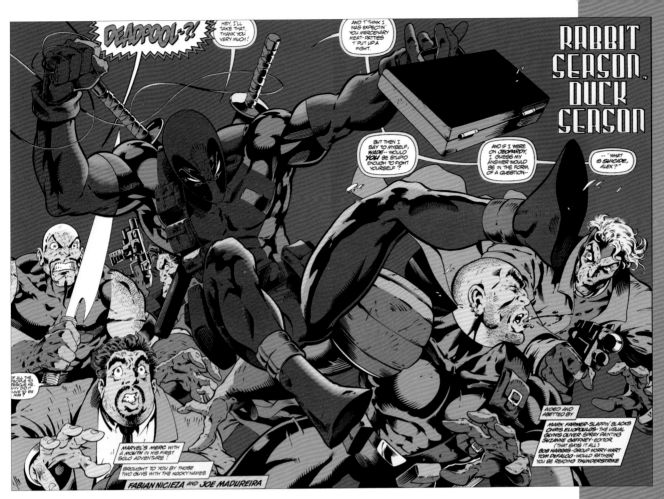

SINS OF THE PAST

Deadpool had a face-off with Killebrew, his creator, teaming up with his old flame Siryn.

*S*ins of the Past (August-November 1994) was the second miniseries dedicated to Deadpool, following on from *The Circle Chase*. A standalone run that wrapped up the first stage of the Merc With a Mouth's life, in these pages Deadpool completed his transition from Super Villain to full on antihero. It was one of the most popular, important stories, and not only because it was the first by Mark Waid, now a hugely popular Marvel writer. "I made a very conscious decision that, in my mind, he was Bugs Bunny," Waid confessed to the website *Vulture*. Without losing any of his irony or insanity, Deadpool was made more human and empathetic. There is a powerful and unforgettable scene where, having lost his

mask, Deadpool is ashamed to show his disfigured face to Siryn, who he was in love with.

The four-part story arc, drawn by Ian Churchill, Ken Lashley, and, in a more classic style, Lee Weeks, started the Deadpool/Siryn pairing. The two of them had to defeat the mutant gangster Black Tom, whom Juggernaut (real name Cain Marko, stepbrother of Professor Charles Xavier) had freed from a government facility to cure the infection that was killing him. To do this, Juggernaut had also kidnapped Doctor Killbrew, who was now attempting to use Deadpool's healing factor to save Black Tom.

At Deadpool's and Siryn's side was Banshee, former X-Men member

and ex-Interpol agent. It was a family event: Banshee (Sean Cassidy) fought his cousin Black Tom alongside his daughter Siryn. The situation was complicated even further by the arrival of Daniel Peyer, an old friend of Banshee, who was convinced that Deadpool had ruined his career.

The story ended with Interpol arresting Black Tom, Deadpool kidnapping Killebrew (the only one who could restore his healing powers), and Peyer, who was still swearing revenge. Take these ingredients and mix in spectacular battle scenes, a little romance and the occasional severed hand, and you have an explosive and entertaining story.

NEXT..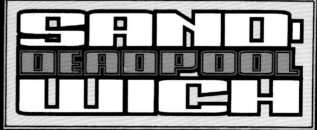

HEY, IT'S DEADPOOL

Deadpool could cope with the Bolivian jungle, Antarctica and a nuclear threat. But being considered one of the good guys was one step too far...

Getting paid with fake money by a revolutionary group. Almost causing an atomic explosion that could wipe out the southern hemisphere. Being considered one of the "good guys" after performing one selfless act. Let's be honest: all that sounds like too much even for Deadpool.

These events from the opening story of his first regular series: 'Hey, It's Deadpool' or *Deadpool #1* (cover date January 1997). Authors Joe Kelly and Ed McGuinness wanted to make the best comic they possibly could, writing and drawing everything that crossed their minds, given that at the time Deadpool was not a big seller. As Kelly revealed to *Bleeding Cool*: "I was told we were canceled almost every third issue and it got to be so ridiculous because I couldn't plan anything. Eventually I left with *issue #33* because I was just tired of being told we would be gone soon."

Luckily, it didn't get canceled at all and since then Deadpool hasn't regularly appeared on

ABOVE:
Cover from *Deadpool #1* (January 1997). Art by Ed McGuinness.

LEFT:
Two pages from "Hey, It's Deadpool" from *Deadpool #1* (January 1997). Script by Joe Kelly. Art by Ed McGuinness (pencils), Nathan Massengill and Norman Lee (inks), Chris Lichtner (colors), Richard Starkings, Comicraft and Dave Lanphear (letters).

newsstands and in comic stores. Kelly laid the foundations for the series right from the beginning. It was clear from the first issue that the story was going to move at a frenzied, whirlwind pace, with Deadpool taking on revolutionary rebels in the Bolivian jungle and then being sent to Antarctica under false pretenses. He had been told him it would be a piece of cake: demolishing an abandoned science facility in an isolated location. Yeah, a real piece of cake…

Unfortunately for Deadpool, there were one or two little problems to contend with. If the sub-zero temperature wasn't bad enough, there was also the fact that the monstrous Alpha Flight member, Walter Langowski /Sasquatch was there waiting for him. Oh, and the core of the nuclear power plant was about to explode. And then, to top it off, it was was revealed that it had all been just a test (which he passed, of course), with a view toward him going on future missions as a "guardian of humanity." What? A test? Guardian of humanity? On the good guys' side? Let's just say our Merc's reaction was much less violent than expected. Maybe he was starting to mellow?

91

ONE OF US

It was a "mission impossible" for the Merc with a Mouth where he infiltrated the Skrull base to trick them — twice.

ABOVE:
A detail of the extraordinary cover of *Deadpool #1* (November 2008). Art by Clayton Crain.

OPPOSITE PAGE, TOP:
How many Deadpools? *Deadpool #3*, "One of Us: Part 2" (December 2008). Script by Daniel Way. Art by Paco Medina (pencils), Juan Vlasco (inks), Marte Gracia (colors), Cory Petit (letters).

When the New Avengers found out that Elektra, the lethal ninja warrior and Daredevil's ex-lover, had been replaced by a Skrull, it seemed fairly clear that the alien warrior civilization was silently infiltrating human (and Super Hero) society to prepare for the final invasion. This was the premise of *Secret Invasion* (2008), an exciting Marvel crossover, written by Brian Michael Bendis and drawn by Leinil Francis Yu.

Deadpool was also mixed up in these events—in his own way, of course. He entered the picture in *One of Us*, a three-part story arc from 2008 by Daniel Way (writer) and Paco Medina (artist). The Merc with a Mouth was dressed up in a bear costume, masquerading as a team mascot, during a baseball game that was interrupted by the arrival of a Skrull spaceship hovering over the diamond. Gaining the invaders' trust, Deadpool managed to get into their base on Mount Cheyenne. There he convinced them to create a generation of Super Skrulls with his healing factor. There was just one detail he didn't share: his DNA also carried madness.

Deadpool was actually on a mission for Nick Fury, who had promised him a big reward if he managed to get information on the Skull Queen Veranke. A Super Skrull (nicknamed "Chilly McHotpants" by Deadpool) discovered him, but the Merc With a Mouth managed to deal with this new foe. But what about the rest of the Super Skrulls? Well, his DNA was actually slowly killing them, his aggressive healing factor twisting the warriors' healthy bodies. Mission complete, the obtained data was sent to Fury, but Norman Osborn intercepted it…

MAGNUM OPUS

Deadpool set out to exact revenge on Norman Osborn, only to end up losing his head (in every sense) over Black Widow.

He shouldn't have messed with Norman Osborn. Deadpool diligently completed the mission to infiltrate the Skrull base, as we saw in '*One of Us*,' but when Osborn got hold of the stolen information on how to kill Skrull Queen Veranke, the Green Goblin became a national hero. Deadpool got neither glory nor money—he even lost the hundred million Nick Fury had offered him as a reward. That's why our Merc with a Mouth was furious with Osborn and planning his revenge.

The only thing was that Osborn wasn't so easy to kill, as Daniel Way, Andy Diggle (writers) and Paco Medina and Bong Dazo (artists) showed us in *Magnum Opus,* one of the most popular Deadpool story arcs. In this spectacular four-part crossover with the *Thunderbolts* that came out in 2009, Deadpool tried out a suicidal tactic: attacking Avengers Tower. It was a plan so crazy it might even have worked, had Norman not already fled the tower, leaving the Thunderbolts there waiting for Deadpool. The Merc was no match for their combined might.

Deadpool fled to find some allies and the Thunderbolts followed after Ant-Man (Eric O'Grady) planted a tracker on him. When they caught up with the Merc they found two Deadpools: one was the real deal, and the other was Taskmasker, his new ally, disguised as the Merc.

The fight was absurd. While the fake Deadpool kept the Thunderbolts busy, the real Deadpool snuck up on Black Widow and surprised her—but instead of killing her he asked her if she had a boyfriend. In response, he got a knee

to the groin. The scuffle between the two Deadpools and the Thunderbolts continued—with a lot of twists and turns (including a kiss stolen from the Widow, who the Merc had fallen in love with)—until the last chapter, when Deadpool was apparently decapitated by the Headsman. Dead? No way!

Once Deadpool had been stitched back together, he went to thank Taskmaster for re-assembling him... only to find out it wasn't the false Deadpool who had done the needlework. Deadpool came to the conclusion that the Widow loved him after all and she had been the one to put him together again.

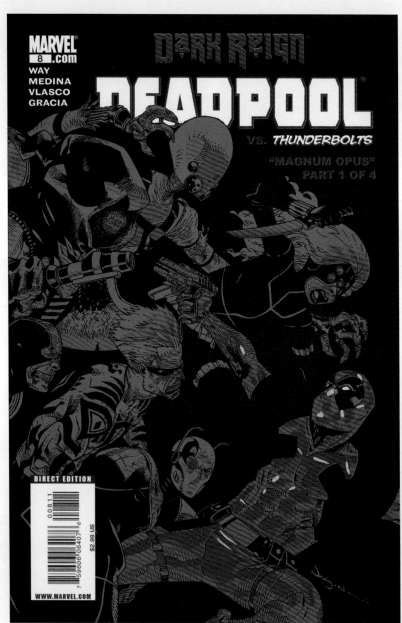

RIGHT:
Cover from *Deadpool #8* (May 2009). Art by Jason Pearson.

STORIES

ABOVE FAR LEFT: Splash-page from *Deadpool #8* (May 2009), "Magnum Opus Part 1: All Your Base Are Belong to Us." Script by Daniel Way. Art by Paco Medina (pencils), Juan Vlasco (inks), Marte Gracia (colors), Cory Petit (letters)

ABOVE LEFT: Are Deadpool and Black Widow (Yelena Belova) friends or enemies? *Deadpool #9* (June 2009) Script by Daniel Way. Art by Paco Medina (pencils), Juan Vlasco (inks), Marte Gracia (colors), Cory Petit (letters).

LEFT: Deadpool falls in love. What a romantic guy! *Thunderbolts #131* (June 2009). Script by Andy Diggle. Art by Bong Dazo (pencils), Joe Pimentel (inks), Frank Martin Jr. and Giovanni Kosoki (colors), Albert Deschesne (letters).

THE GOOD, THE BAD, AND THE UGLY

Cap, Wolverine, and Wade embarked on a mission in North Korea.
Guess who was the ugly one!

ABOVE:
Cover for
Deadpool #15
(October 2013).
Art by Declan
Shalvey &
Jordie Bellaire.

RIGHT:
Wade to
the rescue!
Deadpool #16
(November
2013). Script
by Brian
Posehn & Gerry
Duggan. Art by
Declan Shalvey
(pencils, inks),
Jordie Bellaire
(colors), Joe
Sabino (letters).

**TOP OPPOSITE
PAGE:**
Deadpool
destroys the
North Korean
facility,
Deadpool #19
(January 2014).
Script by Brian
Posehn & Gerry
Duggan. Art by
Declan Shalvey
(pencils, inks),
Jordie Bellaire
(colors), Joe
Sabino (letters).

The acclaimed series 'The Good, the Bad, and the Ugly' is named after Sergio Leone's Western masterpiece. But in this story arc, the Good was Captain America, the Bad was Wolverine and the Ugly was —you've guessed it—Deadpool. The series, which came out in *Deadpool #15* and *#19*, vol. 3 (2013), was written by Gerry Duggan and Brian Pohsen and drawn by Declan Shalvey.

In the first chapter, Wade went off in search of Logan and Steve's help. He was convinced that someone was still experimenting on the Weapon X lab rats. Soon all three of them were kidnapped and brought to Butler's secret laboratory, in a concentration camp in North Korea. Butler, one of the scientists who had experimented on Deadpool, confessed to finding out that Wade's healing factor was a cure for cancer and that his DNA was the key ingredient for creating new Super Soldiers. Butler, in search of a cure for his sick sister, revealed to Wade that he had kidnapped him from time to time to subject him to new experiments, then erased his memory to cover his tracks. This had allowed him to make new mutants, financed by the North Korean government. The lab rats had both the powers of various X-Men and the monstrous appearance caused by Wade's healing factor.

Luckily, one of the victims of the experiments decided to help Deadpool. He was called Kim and he had the demonic appearance of the X-Man Nightcrawler as well as his powers: agility and teleportation. Once Steve and Logan were freed, the group also got the rest of the prisoners to safety. But there was a second camp, where the lab rats' families were imprisoned. Many of them, though, were already dead—including Carmelita Camacho, Wade's ex-girlfriend and the mother of their child, Eleanor, who Wade hadn't known about! Cap helped the mutants and their surviving relatives escape to America, while Deadpool got revenge on Butler.

Back home, Wade placed his little girl into the care of his friend Emily Preston.

DESPICABLE DEADPOOL

Everyone hated Deadpool… and everyone had a good reason!

Was there ever a time in Deadpool's life when he really hit bottom? Maybe somewhere between *issue #287* and *issue #300* of his series. If the numbering seems high, that's because at the time Marvel had launched a new publishing initiative, Marvel Legacy: in which all series were labeled with the numbers they would have had by combining all titles with the same protagonist. During the Marvel Legacy months, the writers also revived aspects of Deadpool's past. And what was the common thread in his past if not being a universally hated antihero? It was a reputation that, in the months prior to these stories, Wade had been trying to move away from.

In the previous issues, Wade had made a huge error in judgment and trusted Captain America. Too bad it was an evil version of Cap: Hydra-Cap's machinations had led to the death of Coulson and Emily Preston, Wade's friend and ally. As a result of Emily's death, Wade's recently discovered daughter, Eleanor, also disowned her father.

Making everything more complicated was a standing debt with the evil Stryfe, who shortly before had helped heal Wade's friends from a virus. Deadpool was forced to repay this debt by attacking Cable and other enemies of Stryfe, until he managed to break free of the blackmail. But now all hope of redemption was lost. After putting a bounty on his own head to wipe himself off the map, and facing old friends like Rogue and Cap (the real one!), Wade decided to start from scratch. He used Butler's technology on himself and erased his own memory. The last story arc of Gerry Duggan's long run ended with a Wade without any recent memories (including the memory of Eleanor) and ready to restart his career as a mercenary.

RIGHT:
Deadpool steals Cable's metal arm. *Despicable Deadpool #287* (December 2017). Script by Gerry Duggan. Art by Scott Koblish (pencils, inks), Nick Filardi (colors), Joe Sabino (letters).

TOP LEFT:
Cover for *Despicable Deadpool #291* (February 2018). Art by David Lopez.

LEFT:
Deadpool is ready to start a new life. *Despicable Deadpool #300* (July 2018). Script by Gerry Duggan. Art by Mike Hawthorne (pencils, inks), Nick Filardi (colors), Joe Sabino (letters).

DEADPOOL KILLS THE MARVEL UNIVERSE

Deadpool was able to kill all the heroes in the Marvel Universe. Luckily it was just a parallel world…

The *What If…?* stories tell Marvel adventures set in parallel worlds. Introduced by Uatu the Watcher, they answer questions about what would have happened if the lives of our favorite characters had gone down a different path. In a similar vein, the miniseries *Deadpool Kills the Marvel Universe* (2012), written by Cullen Bunn and drawn in dark tones by Dalibor Talajić, answers a simple, disturbing question: what would happen if Deadpool declared war on the heroes (and criminals) of the Marvel Universe?

Corrupted by the mental manipulations of Psycho-Man, the despot of the Microverse, Deadpool set out to annihilate all the super beings. In creative and often unpredictable ways, he killed all the Avengers, the X-Men, Spider-Man, and even vigilantes like Punisher, unstoppable beings like Hulk, and villains like Venom and Goblin. To stop him, the heroes' loved ones hired the mercenary Taskmaster, one of the most lethal on the market.

In the finale, Deadpool—or rather, "Dreadpool," as writer Cullen Bunn rebaptized him, at first only in interviews—fought Taskmaster in the Nexus of All Realities. Deadpool defeated Taskmaster, inadvertently helped by Man-Thing, the guardian of the Nexus. But then he also killed the monster, and went through the portal that connects all the worlds in the Multiverse. On the final page, Wade ended up in our world, in the Marvel offices… ready to kill his creators!

The miniseries was such a success that it led to several sequels: *Deadpool Killustrated*, *Deadpool Kills Deadpool*, and *Deadpool Kills the Marvel Universe Again*.

RIGHT:
Cover for *Deadpool Kills the Marvel Universe #1* (October 2012). Art by Kaare Andrews.

TOP AND BOTTOM FAR LEFT: With a single strike, Deadpool eliminated almost all the Avengers. *Deadpool Kills the Marvel Universe #2* (October 2012). Script by Cullen Bunn. Art by Dalibor Talajic (pencils, inks), Lee Loughridge (colors), Joe Sabino (letters)

ABOVE: Cover for *Deadpool Kills the Marvel Universe #3* (August 2012). Art by Kaare Andrews.

LEFT: Cover for *Deadpool Kills the Marvel Universe #4* (October 2012). Art by Kaare Andrews.

EXTRA

CREATORS

ROB LIEFELD

The bad boy of the US comic scene in the '90s wanted to write about Spider-Man and Wolverine—which is how he ended up creating Deadpool and Cable.

"Wolverine was unaccessible, Spider-Man was unaccessible, those books were protecting those characters. So the reason *New Mutants* was attractive to me was I could fix it up, I could change it," Rob Liefeld revealed to *Forbes* magazine in 2016. He was jealous of his colleagues Todd McFarlane, Erik Larsen, and other artists who were writing for and drawing the wall-crawler and the clawed mutant. He couldn't. So all he could do was create a "personal" Spider-Man and Wolverine—which is how Deadpool and Cable ended up appearing in *The New Mutants.* It was the lowest-selling mutant comic series at the time, but in 1991, thanks to the three legendary *issues #98, #99, and #100,* Liefeld turned it into a commercial success, in collaboration with writer Fabian Nicieza.

It was the '90s, a decade in which young creators injected classic titles with a bold new style—though it was also arguably a time of style over substance. Artists Liefeld, McFarlane, Silvestri, Lee, Larsen, Valentino, and Portacio—household names in the world of comics—were taking over the market with their hypertrophic, exaggerated versions of Super Heroes. In 1992, they decided to cut ties with the "Big Two" (Marvel and DC), where they had become stars, to found their own company: Image Comics.

Liefeld might be the most controversial, loved, hated, celebrated, and talked-about of them all, with his exaggerated, distorted bodies, and his taste for over-the-top narrative, splash pages, and breaking out of the panel "cages." He managed to capture the spirit of the times. Born in Anheim, California, in 1967, Liefeld was the son of a Baptist pastor and a secretary, with a passion for comics and dreams of becoming an artist. But Liefeld was shy—he wasn't brave enough to share his work. A friend convinced him to go to a convention and introduce himself to Dick Giordano (DC) and

Mark Gruenwald (Marvel). The two legendary editors saw the novelty and freshness in his sketches and panels, and started to give him projects: *Hawke and Dove* for the Distinguished Competition and none other than *The New Mutants* (from *issue #86*) for the House of Ideas. Liefeld's breakthrough was when he took over control of the latter series in *issue #98,* along with Nicieza.

Liefeld turned into a rock star in the comics world, even appearing in a spot for Levi's jeans directed by Spike Lee, and he became a millionaire. Some criticized his work, but other writers such as Grant Morrison and Robert Kirkman fondly recalled his style, energy, and enthusiasm.

After a great start, *Youngblood, Bloodstrike,* and the other titles from his studio Extreme (within Image) failed to achieve success and missed publishing deadlines. In 1996 Liefeld left Image, and that same year he signed with Marvel to do *The Avengers and Captain America* for the Heroes Reborn project.

In the 2000s he founded the new independent studio Awesome, and then Arcade Comics, but he went back to work for Marvel multiple times. In 2010 he picked up Deadpool again, drawing *issue #1* of *Prelude to Deadpool Corps* and the first nine issues of *Deadpool Corps.* Later on he even had a cameo in the Merc with a Mouth's first movie, and in 2021 he returned to Marvel to celebrate thirty years of Deadpool, drawing the thirty variant covers of *Deadpool Nerdy 30.*

FABIAN NICIEZA

This celebrated writer set out to make Deadpool a "pain in the ass!"

"Deadpool was described to me as Spider-Man crossed with Punisher," co-creator Fabian Nicieza said in an interview on the Spanish language website *Hipertextual,* recalling the creation of the Merc with a Mouth in 1993's *The New Mutants.* "Making him act like an annoying pain in the ass was something that helped set him apart from the star of *The New Mutants,* Cable, plus it was different from the usual way of portraying a mercenary. I made him act like an idiot, and the readers loved it."

Nicieza was born in Buenos Aires, Argentina, in 1961. When he was four he moved with his family to the USA —to New Jersey. He joined Marvel in 1985 to work on the editorial staff. He started to write articles for the magazine *Marvel Age.* In '87 his first script was published (*Psi-Force*). Then he was put in charge of the text for *The New Warriors,* which he considered one of his best productions. His other works include *Alpha Flight, The Avengers,* and the stunning miniseries *The Adventures of Captain America* (with artist Kevin Maguire).

Nicieza penned the dialogue for the final three issues of *The New Mutants* along with artist (and co-plotter) Rob Liefeld, where the two of them invented Deadpool. They also created the staggeringly successful *X-Force*—its first issue alone sold five million copies.

That success led Nicieza to work on

about Deadpool, but the character's other creator, Rob Liefeld, had left the House of Ideas to try out Image. A new artist was needed. The job was offered to Joe Madureira of Philadelphia, Pennsylvania, barely 19 at the time (though he had been an intern at Marvel since he was 16. He had already created the art for two short stories in *Marvel Comics Presents* and two episodes of *Excalibur*. His new miniseries was called *The Circle Chase* and it definitively made the Merc with a Mouth one of the most popular Marvel heroes.

Joe "Mad" Madureira won everyone over with his over-the-top, hyperrealist style, which was reminiscent of an extreme version of the work of Arthur Adams, though Madureira was also clearly influenced by Manga and video games. He was an expert on the latter, and at the end of the decade Madureira temporarily abandoned comics for games, only to return later.

Deadpool was the first of many jobs he took on for Marvel, which also included *Uncanny X-Men, Astonishing X-Men, Ultimates, Avenging Spider-Man, Savage Wolverine,* and *Inhumans.*

---

the most important mutant titles. In 1992 he moved on to *X-Men*, picking up where Chris Claremont left off and penning a three-year run, but he didn't abandon other characters like Cable and Deadpool. In 1993, Nicieza wrote the first miniseries for the latter character, *The Circle Chase*, which was drawn by Joe Madureira.

MARK WAID

The comics veteran who revealed the first truths about Deadpool.

Born in 1962, Waid has written stories for the most famous and popular characters in the Marvel universe (X-Men, Fantastic Four, Avengers, Black Widow, Daredevil, Spider-Man, Hulk) and DC (Flash, JLA, Superman). After writing for the magazine *Amazing Heroes* in the 1980s, Waid was hired as an editor at DC Comics in 1987. In 1992, he embarked on writing a popular run of *The Flash*.

After he moved to Marvel in 1994, he was soon assigned a character who was already a fan favorite: Deadpool, who until then had only been the star of one miniseries, *The Circle Chase.* Deadpool was a blank slate on which a whole mythology could be built. Waid, along with artist Ian Churchill, wrote the second miniseries starring Wade: *Sins of the Past.* Accompanied by the red-headed heroine Siryn, Deadpool fought Juggernaut and Black Tom and tracked down Dr. Emrys Killebrew, the man who was

responsible for turning Wade Wilson into Deadpool.

JOE MADUREIRA

A talented artist who was almost as "Mad" as the Merc with a Mouth!

It was 1993. Fabian Nicieza had been hired to write the first miniseries

JOE KELLY

Deadpool's other dad — the writer who turned Deadpool from a bit player into a superstar.

When Deadpool took his first steps, his creators Rob Liefeld and Fabian Nicieza held his hands. But there's a writer we could call Wade's adoptive father, who inherited Liefeld and Nicieza's legacy… though we don't know how happy he was about that responsibility!

Joe Kelly's career in comics started after he participated in a Marvel-led recruitment campaign for emerging talents at universities.

His first major job came in 1997 when he was entrusted with the launch of the first ongoing *Deadpool* series. Before then, Wade had only appeared in other titles as a guest or a miniseries protagonist. This time, he was the main event. The title paired Kelly with another near-rookie, artist Ed McGuinness. The series—which Kelly wrote until 1999— was a success, maybe an unexpected one. The stories marked the debuts of characters destined to join the main cast of Deadpool comics to come, like the villain T-Ray and Deadpool's ally Blind Al. Once he'd left Deadpool behind, Kelly busied himself with *Daredevil* and *X-Men*, before working for DC Comics on the prestigious *Action Comics* title, chronicled the adventures of Superman from 1999 to 2004. He later worked on other titles such as *JLA* and *Superboy*.

He went back to Marvel at the end of the 2000s and joined the team of creators who took turns working on *Amazing Spider-Man* for a few years. Kelly has been involved in multimedia projects for some time. His independent series *I Kill Giants*, created with J.M. Ken Nimura, was turned into a film produced by Netflix. Along with Joe Casey, Duncan Rouleau, and Steven T. Seagle he founded the studio Man of Action, which among other things can boast the creation of the popular cartoon *Ben 10*. But despite all these projects, Kelly couldn't keep away from Wade Wilson, and in 2016 he went back to write more of his adventures in the series *Spider-Man/Deadpool*.

ED MCGUINNESS

His over the top, unique work on *Vampirella* inspired Marvel to give him Deadpool!

The career of Massachuesetts-born artist Ed McGuinness career took off at the end of the '90s, when he drew the beautiful *Vampirella*. His original style — over-the-top and powerful, inspired by past greats like Jack Kirby and Arthur Adams, and clearly influenced by manga — did not go unnoticed by Marvel. In 1997 they asked him to work on the new regular series of *Deadpool* scripted by Joe Kelly. McGuinness has worked for the House of Ideas ever since.

The list of Super Heroes that McGuinness has drawn is impressive: X-Men, the Avengers, Cable, Captain America, Guardians of the Galaxy, Nova. But his name is most associated with Deadpool and the Incredible Hulk. McGuinness created Red Hulk in the series dedicated to the green giant, and drew the first nine comics of the Merc with a Mouth's regular series. Then, in 2016, still with Joe Kelly writing, he illustrated a dozen episodes of the series *Spider-Man/Deadpool*. Looks like he really can't live without the Merc with a Mouth…

DANIEL WAY

The writer who even convinced Nick Fury to trust Deadpool, in order to defeat the Skrulls.

Born in Michigan in 1974, Daniel Way won the Xeric Grant for indie comics in 2000 for his project *Violent Lifestyle*, so he was destined to write *Deadpool* someday! After that prize, he was hired by Marvel to script some short stories about Spider-Man in *Tangled Web*. Then he was assigned the text for *Agent X, Venom, Bullseye, Hulk, Wolverine, and Ghost Rider*. In *Wolverine: Origins*, Way brought back the Merc with a Mouth. So, in 2008, he was chosen (along with artist Paco Medina) to launch the new *Deadpool*

series. Some of his most important projects include the story arcs 'One of Us' and 'Magnum Opus.'

In an interview on the website *CBR.com*, Way explained why Fury unexpectedly hires Deadpool to infiltrate the Skrull base: "Let's say Nick Fury sends in a good guy. The Skrulls have been watching us for some time now and they're going to know it's completely out of character and out of that guy's moral comfort zone. If Fury sends a bad guy… There are defectors and Deadpool is a great candidate to be one. He's pretty morally ambiguous, has no real loyalties." Makes it all clearer, doesn't it?

PACO MEDINA

This talented Mexican artist has worked on some of the most important *Deadpool* story arcs.

In 2003 Paco Medina had just left the Distinguished Competition and was looking for work. As he told *Forbes Mexico*: "Without even meeting Joe Quesada [then Editor in chief of Marvel], I sent him copies of my drawings saying that I was Mexican, that I'd worked for DC, and that I was looking for new opportunities… I think I was very lucky: he liked my work." So much so, that Quesada trusted him with some of the most important characters from the House of Ideas: Thor, Fantastic Four, Wolverine, Spider-Man, X-Men, Ultimate X-Men, Venom, the Avengers, New Warriors, and, best of all, Deadpool, his favorite (along with Wolverine).

For Medina it has been a treat to draw the Merc with a Mouth's story cycles, often collaborating with writer Daniel Way: *One of Us, Horror Business, How Low Can You Go?, Magnum Opus, Bullseye, Want You to Want Me*. A treat like when, one day in kindergarten in Mexico, his teacher told him and his classmates to try painting on an easel. Francisco "Paco" Medina hasn't stopped since.

VICTOR GISCHLER

This acclaimed author is the writer of the maxiseries *Deadpool: Merc with a Mouth.*

What do Punisher, Deadpool, and Dracula have in common? Well, the first two have a few screws loose and a decent supply of weapons, while the last two have a wife in common (don't ask…). And all three of the characters have had adventures written by Victor Gischler. Born in 1969 and hailing from Baton Rouge, Louisiana, he is the author of several novels which have been nominated for the Edgar, Anthony, and Bram Stoker Awards. His stories have often been hard-boiled noir, but thanks to his work for Marvel he has proved he knows how to move between genres.

Gischler is the writer of a famous maxiseries, *Deadpool: Merc with a Mouth,* in which Wade ended up having strange adventures with the zombie head of a Deadpool from a parallel world: Headpool! Gischler also wrote the series *Deadpool Corps,* drawn by Rob Liefeld, where he created a bunch of alternate versions of Wade, such as Lady Deadpool, Major Deadpool, amongst others! Throughout his career, Gischler has also written different stories about the X-Men, including the 'Curse of the Mutants' saga, where they took on vampires!

GERRY DUGGAN & BRIAN POSEHN

These writers turned Deadpool's life upside down.

There's one writer at the top of the Deadpool "mountain." His name is Gerry Duggan, and he's the one who has written the most Deadpool stories overall. "It really feels like Deadpool was a mountain that was built slowly by others over the years," he said in an interview with *CBR.com*. "The folks that came before me made him popular and then I sort of got to walk up and do my thing at the top of a mountain."

Before becoming a comics writer, Duggan worked in a comic book store in Hollywood, Golden Apple Comics. He was also the writer and producer of the live television show *Attack of the Show!*

Duggan started writing *Deadpool* in 2013 along with Brian Posehn, also the writer of several episodes of *Attack of the Show!* and of the Image Comics series *The Last Christmas*. Posehn also had a varied career as a stand-up comedian, actor, and musician. You might know him as geologist Bert Kibbler in *The Big Bang Theory*, Brian Supowski in *The Sarah Silverman Program*, or the creepy biology professor in *New Girl*. Duggan and Posehn were the perfect combination to launch the *Deadpool* series and turn it into a huge success, starting with their first story arc, which saw Wade take on the zombie presidents of the USA.

This was the start of a very long run and Duggan kept writing the series even after Posehn left, until 2019. During this time he wrote some of the most popular recent stories about Deadpool, explored his most tragic side, had him fight alongside both Dr. Strange and Captain America, made him a member of the Avengers, had him marry Shiklah, the queen of the monsters, and had him battle zombie American presidents. Duggan even appeared in the last issue he wrote, in which Wade stole his car. Today he's busy with several X-Men titles, but every so often he thinks back to Deadpool: "I hope I'll have been as good to Wade as he was to me."

MIKE HAWTHORNE

The Deadpool record holder.

There's one artist with a special place in Deadpool fans' hearts: Mike Hawthorne. Hailing from York, Pennsylvania, he's the one who has drawn the most stories about the character overall. The first encounter between the artist and Wade was in 2013, in *Deadpool #8 Vol.3*. Hawthorne was asked to draw a story arc of the series that had been relaunched a few months earlier by

Duggan, Posehn, and Tony Moore. It wasn't an easy task: in the earlier issues, Deadpool's crazy adventures had been illustrated in a grotesque, meticulous style by Moore.

Since then, the artist has illustrated almost forty issues of Deadpool across three different series. Jordan D. White, the editor of all the issues drawn by Mike, told *Marvel.com*, "He's taken Deadpool up against S.H.I.E.L.D., got him married, made him rich, gave him a new arch-nemesis, shot him into space, and much, much more! He's been a dream to work with." In the last few years, Hawthorne has drawn issues of *Superior Spider-Man* and *Daredevil*.

DEADPOOL'S OTHER CREATORS

An incomplete list...

In Deadpool's thirty years of existence, many writers and artists have tried their hand at working with the Merc with a Mouth. Kelly Thompson, writer for the *Captain Marvel* and *Black Widow* series, wrote the most recent ongoing *Deadpool* title. For the first issues she was accompanied by Chris Bachalo, with his explosive, original style. She wasn't the only female writer to take on Wade: Gail Simone wrote *Deadpool* in 2002, from *#65* to *#69*, and then *Agent X*.

In the last decade, many artists have taken turns drawing for the various series about Wade: among them Matteo Lolli, Scott Koblish (artist of the genius "flashback" stories) and cover artists like Dave Johnson and Mark Brooks. An artist behind many special projects starring Wade is Salva Espin, who drew the miniseries *Secret Agent: Deadpool, Deadpool vs. Carnage, You Are Deadpool,* and the spin-off *Deadpool & the Mercs for Money.*

In 2018 writer/artist Skottie Young relaunched *Deadpool*, teaming up with the artist Nic Klein. And we can't forget David Lapham and Kyle Baker, who were behind the maxiseries *Deadpool MAX*. Some of the others who have worked on Deadpool in the 2000s include writer Christopher Priest and artists Scott McDaniel, Paco Diaz, and Pete Woods.

MARVEL STUDIOS LIBRARY

MOVIE SPECIALS
- MARVEL STUDIOS' *SPIDER-MAN FAR FROM HOME*
- MARVEL STUDIOS' *ANT-MAN AND THE WASP*
- MARVEL STUDIOS' *AVENGERS: ENDGAME*
- MARVEL STUDIOS' *AVENGERS: INFINITY WAR*
- MARVEL STUDIOS' *BLACK PANTHER* (COMPANION)
- MARVEL STUDIOS' *BLACK WIDOW*
- MARVEL STUDIOS' *CAPTAIN MARVEL*
- MARVEL STUDIOS: THE FIRST TEN YEARS
- MARVEL STUDIOS' *THOR: RAGNAROK*
- MARVEL STUDIOS' *AVENGERS*: AN INSIDER'S GUIDE TO THE AVENGERS' FILMS

MARVEL STUDIOS' BLACK WIDOW: THE OFFICIAL MOVIE SPECIAL

MARVEL STUDIOS' THE FALCON AND THE WINTER SOLDIER: THE OFFICIAL MARVEL STUDIOS COLLECTOR SPECIAL

MARVEL STUDIOS' WANDAVISION THE OFFICIAL MARVEL STUDIOS COLLECTOR SPECIAL

STAR WARS LIBRARY

STAR WARS: THE EMPIRE STRIKES BACK: THE 40TH ANNIVERSARY SPECIAL EDITION

STAR WARS: THE MANDALORIAN GUIDE TO SEASON ONE

STAR WARS INSIDER: THE FICTION COLLECTION VOLUME 2

STAR WARS: THE SKYWALKER SAGA THE OFFICIAL COLLECTOR'S EDITION

- *ROGUE ONE: A STAR WARS STORY* THE OFFICIAL COLLECTOR'S EDITION
- *ROGUE ONE: A STAR WARS STORY* THE OFFICIAL MISSION DEBRIEF
- *STAR WARS: THE LAST JEDI* THE OFFICIAL COLLECTOR'S EDITION
- *STAR WARS: THE LAST JEDI* THE OFFICIAL MOVIE COMPANION
- *STAR WARS: THE LAST JEDI* THE ULTIMATE GUIDE

- *SOLO: A STAR WARS STORY* THE OFFICIAL COLLECTOR'S EDITION
- *SOLO: A STAR WARS STORY* THE ULTIMATE GUIDE
- **THE BEST OF** *STAR WARS INSIDER* VOLUME 1
- **THE BEST OF** *STAR WARS INSIDER* VOLUME 2
- **THE BEST OF** *STAR WARS INSIDER* VOLUME 3
- **THE BEST OF** *STAR WARS INSIDER* VOLUME 4
- *STAR WARS:* LORDS OF THE SITH
- *STAR WARS:* HEROES OF THE FORCE

- *STAR WARS:* ICONS OF THE GALAXY
- *STAR WARS:* THE SAGA BEGINS
- *STAR WARS* THE ORIGINAL TRILOGY
- *STAR WARS:* ROGUES, SCOUNDRELS AND BOUNTY HUNTERS
- *STAR WARS:* CREATURES, ALIENS, AND DROIDS
- *STAR WARS: THE RISE OF SKYWALKER* THE OFFICIAL COLLECTOR'S EDITION
- *STAR WARS: THE MANDALORIAN:* GUIDE TO SEASON ONE

- *STAR WARS: THE EMPIRE STRIKES BACK* THE 40TH ANNIVERSARY SPECIAL EDITION
- *STAR WARS: AGE OF RESISTANCE* THE OFFICIAL COLLECTORS' EDITION
- *STAR WARS: THE SKYWALKER SAGA* THE OFFICIAL COLLECTOR'S EDITION
- *STAR WARS INSIDER: FICTION COLLECTION* VOLUME 1
- *STAR WARS INSIDER: FICTION COLLECTION* VOLUME 2

MARVEL LEGACY LIBRARY

MARVEL CLASSIC NOVELS
- **WOLVERINE** WEAPON X OMNIBUS
- **SPIDER-MAN** THE DARKEST HOURS OMNIBUS
- **SPIDER-MAN** THE VENOM FACTOR OMNIBUS
- **X-MEN AND THE AVENGERS** GAMMA QUEST OMNIBUS
- **X-MEN** MUTANT EMPIRE OMNIBUS

NOVELS
- **MARVEL'S GUARDIANS OF THE GALAXY** NO GUTS, NO GLORY
- **SPIDER-MAN MILES MORALES** WINGS OF FURY
- **MORBIUS** THE LIVING VAMPIRE: BLOOD TIES
- **ANT-MAN** NATURAL ENEMY
- **AVENGERS** EVERYBODY WANTS TO RULE THE WORLD
- **AVENGERS** INFINITY
- **BLACK PANTHER** WHO IS THE BLACK PANTHER?
- **CAPTAIN AMERICA** DARK DESIGNS
- **CAPTAIN MARVEL** LIBERATION RUN
- **CIVIL WAR**
- **DEADPOOL** PAWS
- **SPIDER-MAN** FOREVER YOUNG
- **SPIDER-MAN** KRAVEN'S LAST HUNT
- **THANOS** DEATH SENTENCE
- **VENOM** LETHAL PROTECTOR
- **X-MEN** DAYS OF FUTURE PAST

THE GUARDIANS OF THE GALAXY THE ART OF THE GAME

MARVEL'S AVENGERS BLACK PANTHER: WAR FOR WAKANDA: THE ART OF THE EXPANSION

MARVEL'S CAPTAIN AMERICA: THE FIRST 80 YEARS

MARVEL: THE FIRST 80 YEARS

- **X-MEN** THE DARK PHOENIX SAGA
- **SPIDER-MAN** HOSTILE TAKEOVER

ART BOOKS
- *THE GUARDIANS OF THE GALAXY* THE ART OF THE GAME

- **MARVEL'S AVENGERS:** *BLACK PANTHER: WAR FOR WAKANDA* THE ART OF THE EXPANSION
- **MARVEL'S** *SPIDER-MAN MILES MORALES* THE ART OF THE GAME
- **MARVEL'S** *AVENGERS* THE ART OF THE GAME
- **MARVEL'S** *SPIDER-MAN* THE ART OF THE GAME

- **MARVEL** *CONTEST OF CHAMPIONS* THE ART OF THE BATTLEREALM
- *SPIDER-MAN: INTO THE SPIDER-VERSE* THE ART OF THE MOVIE
- **THE ART OF IRON MAN** THE ART OF THE MOVIE